THE BIBLE OF RECIPES

SOUS VIDE

2 IN 1

100+ EASY, HEALTHY AND DELICIOUS RECIPES

LUIS JORDAN, HOLLY PORTER

Sommario

SOUS VIDE MADE SIMPLE

50 SIMPLE RECIPES

HOLLY PORTER

INTRODUCTION

Sous vide(French) also known as low temperature long time cooking, is a method of cooking in which food is placed in a plastic pouch or a glass jar and cooked in a water bath for longer than usual cooking times (usually 1 to 7 hours, up to 72 or more hours in some cases) at a precisely regulated temperature.

Sous vide cooking is mostly done using thermal immersion circulator machines. The temperature is much lower than usually used for cooking, typically around 55 to 60 °C (130 to 140 °F) for red meat, 66 to 71 °C (150 to 160 °F) for poultry, and higher for vegetables. The intent is to cook the item evenly, ensuring that the inside is properly cooked without overcooking the outside, and to retain moisture.

Sous vide cooking is much easier than you might think, and usually involved three simple steps:

- Attach your precision cooker to a pot of water and set the time and temperature according to your desired level of doneness.
- Put your food in a sealable bag and clip it to the side of the pot.
- Finish by searing, grilling, or broiling the food to add a crispy, golden exterior layer.

With precise temperature control in the kitchen, sous vide provides the following benefits:

- Consistency. Because you cook your food to a precise temperature for a precise amount of time, you can expect very consistent results.

- Taste. Food cooks in its juices. This ensures that the food is moist, juicy and tender.
- Waste reduction. Traditionally prepared food dries out and results in waste. For example, on average, traditionally cooked steak loses up to 40% of its volume due to drying out. Steak cooked via precision cooking, loses none of its volume.
- Flexibility. Traditional cooking can require your constant attention. Precision cooking brings food to an exact temperature and holds it. There is no worry about overcooking.

- **Roll roast in the bacon net**

Ingredients for 10 portions

- 4 kg pork loin
- 2 pack Cream cheese (cream cheese wreath)
- Pepper
- 2 Onion
- 6 tbsp. Rub (paprika rub) or spices of your choice
- 500 g Bacon, sliced, the slightly thicker
- 200 g Cheddar cheese, in one piece
- 250 g ground beef
- 250 ml Barbecue Sauce

Preparation

Total time approx. 2 days 1 hour 30 minutes

You will need kitchen twine for tying, a sous vide cooker and a vacuum sealer including sealing foil.

Cut the pork salmon with a butterfly cut so that a nice large, flat meat slice is created (to take this step closer would go beyond the scope. There are numerous videos on the Internet, where this is described very nicely. It is really not rocket science). If necessary, tap again with the meat tenderizer or a saucepan like a schnitzel.

In the meantime, cut the onions into strips or rings and put them in a bowl. Add two tablespoons of the spice mixture and knead thoroughly until the onions lose their rigid structure. Spread the remaining rub on the meat surface. Spread the entire cream cheese over the surface of the meat and smooth out. Approximately Remove 18 strips of bacon from the packaging and spread them side by side on the cream cheese. Spread the seasoned onions over the entire surface. Cut approx. 2.5 - 3 cm wide, elongated strips from the block of cheese. Place this on one of the two longer sides on the edge of the meat surface. Roll up the meat surface starting from the cheddar cheese into a sausage in a tight manner and with a little pressure. Tie the roast in about 4 places with kitchen twine so that it does not fall apart.

Place the roast in the sealing bag and vacuum. Approximately Cook for 24 hours in a sous vide bath at 60 ° C.

The next day, lay a bacon net out of the rest of the bacon (my tip with the internet video also applies here). Roll the roast in it. Seal the ends with the minced meat seasoned with rub so that the melted cheese cannot run out. Brush with barbecue sauce.

Fry in the oven preheated to 150 ° C on the grate of the middle rail. It is advisable to slide a baking sheet under the wire rack to catch dripping sauce and fat. After about 30 minutes, glaze the roast again. After another 30 minutes, the sauce is dried to a glossy finish and the roast is ready.

The last step can also be carried out with indirect heat on the charcoal or gas grill. I did this myself and smoked the roast in the meantime. However, the variant with the oven is almost as tasty.

- **Chicken breast in mustard-herb**

Ingredients for 4 portions
For the meat:
- 2 large ones Skinless chicken breasts
- 1 Garlic cloves
- 1 Rosemary
- 3 bay leaves
- 25 g butter
- Sea salt and pepper
For the sauce:
- 25 g butter
- 1 small Onion
- 1 small Garlic cloves
- 2 tbsp. Flour
- 50 ml White wine, drier
- 250 ml chicken stock
- 5 saffron threads
- 200 ml cream

- Herbs, mixed, of your choice
- 1 teaspoon mustard
- Food starch
- Sugar
- Lemon juice
- Salt and pepper
- 2 disc Gouda, middle ages

Preparation

Total time approx. 1 hour 23 minutes

Preheat the Sous Vide bath to 65 ° C.

Halve chicken breasts lengthways so that two small cutlets are created. Salt, pepper and put in a sous vide bag. Peel and slice the garlic. Spread together with the rosemary, bay leaves and butter on the meat. Vacuum everything and 30 min. Cook in a water bath.

Melt the butter and braise the finely chopped onions and garlic until translucent. Dust with the flour and deglaze with white wine and broth. Add saffron and everything about 15 min. simmer over low heat. Remove the meat from the Sous Vide bath and the bag and place in a baking dish.

Add the cream, herbs and mustard to the sauce. Pour the stock from the bag through a fine hair strainer into the sauce, if necessary, tie with starch and season with salt, pepper, sugar and lemon juice. If you want, you can only add the herbs at the very end and briefly puree the sauce beforehand.

Pour a little sauce over the meat, it should not be completely covered and covered with half a slice of cheese for about 7 - 8 min. cook at full top heat.

Serve the remaining sauce extra.

It goes well with rice and salad, but also potatoes or pasta.

- **Lamb sous-vide - without searing**

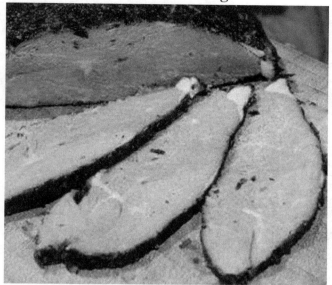

Ingredients for 4 portions
- 4 Lamb hips, 180 g each
- 3 tbsp. heapedherbs of Provence
- 2 tbsp. olive oil

Preparation

Total time approx. 2 hours 10 minutes

Preheat a sous vide suitable oven to 54 ° C.

First turn the lamb hips in the herbs, then put the oil in a bag suitable for sous vide and vacuum. The meat should be at room temperature.

Let it cook in a water bath for 2 hours.

Tip: A pleasure even when cold.

- **Pulpo in chorizo butter**

Ingredients for 4 portions
- 400 g Octopus, (Pulpo), ready to cook
- 1 Cloves of garlic, in large slices
- 1 Bay leaf
- 50 ml Red wine, dry
- 2 tbsp. olive oil
- 1 large Bell pepper, red
- 200 g Cherry tomato, halved
- 100 g butter
- 100 g Chorizo, in thin slices
- 1 Clove of garlic, finely diced
- Smoked salt
- Chili powder
- Sea-salt
- Oil

Preparation

Total time approx. 2 hours 20 minutes

Roast the peppers in an oven heated to 200 ° C until the skin turns black and is easy to remove. Roughly dice the peeled and pitted peppers and set the oven to 150 ° C. Halve the cherry tomatoes, place the cut surface on a well-oiled baking sheet, sprinkle with sea salt and put in the oven.

Vacuum the pulpo together with the garlic slices, bay leaf, red wine and olive oil and place in a water bath heated to 72 ° C (sous-vide bath). Pulpo and tomatoes both take about 1.5 hours.

Shortly before the end of the cooking time, melt the butter in a pan that is not too hot and lightly roast the chorizo slices and the garlic cubes. Add paprika powder, paprika cubes and cherry tomatoes, mix carefully and season with smoked salt and chilli powder, then remove from the fire.

Remove the pulpo from the brew, pat dry, cut into slices about 5 mm thick and add to the chorizo butter.

To fit : fresh baguette, rosemary baked potatoes, ravioli filled with bacon and ricotta.

Since a pulpo usually weighs far more than 400 g, several servings can be cooked in the sous-vide bath at the same time, cooled down in ice water for at least 10 minutes and then quickly frozen. If necessary, regenerate in a 70 ° C hot bath.

- **Spinach quail**

Ingredients for 1 portions
- 1 Quail
- 1 Chicken breast fillet
- 50 g Spinach, blanched
- 150 ml cream
- 100 g sauerkraut
- 20 g Carrot, diced finely
- 20 g Sugar snap
- 10 g Horseradish, fresh
- 4 small ones Potato, cook floury, already cooked
- Herbs to taste
- Salt and pepper
- Clarified butter
  Preparation

Total time approx. 2 hours

Cut the chicken breast into pieces and puree with the spinach. Season the farce with salt and pepper.

Detach the quail meat from the bone and lightly salt it. Spread the breasts on a vacuum wrap. Spread the spinach farce on top and cover everything with the quail legs. Wrap in the film and form into a roll. Now vacuum the roll and place it in a water bath at 58 ° C. Let it steep in about 1 hour.

In the meantime, warm the fresh sauerkraut with the cream, add the blanched and cubed carrots, the sugar snap peas and the boiled potatoes. Bring everything to the boil briefly and then season with horseradish.

Remove the foil from the quail roll. Briefly fry the roll with herbs all around.

Cut into slices and serve.

- Turkey breast cut in pepper coat

Ingredients for 4 portions

- 1 kg turkey breast
- 6 tbsp. pepper Steak
- 2 tbsp. raw cane sugar

Preparation

Total time approx. 6 hours

Mix the steak pepper and raw sugar. Turn the turkey breast in the mixture and press down well. Vacuum everything in one bag. Preheat the sous-vide device to 80 degrees. Place the bag in the water bath for approx. 4 hours.

Take out and let cool in the bag. When the turkey breast is cold, pat dry, cut into thin slices (cold cuts).

Goes well with asparagus.

- **Salmon with capers on a salad**

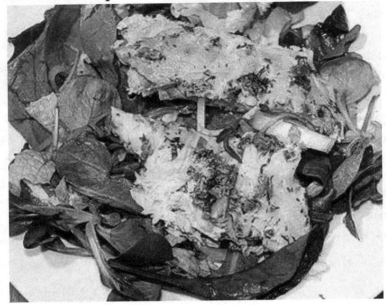

Ingredients for 2 portions
- 300 g Salmon fillet without skin
- 2 tbsp. capers
- ½ bundle dill
- 1 bag Lettuce, mixed
- 1 m Onion, red
- 2 tbsp. Balsamic, dark
- 1 tbsp. fish sauce
- 1 tbsp. Olive oil
- 1 teaspoon pepper

Preparation

Total time approx. 50 minutes

Finely chop 1 tbsp. capers and the dill. Rub the salmon in with this mixture. Put the salmon in a sous vide bag and in a water bath at 55 degrees for 35 min. ferment.

Cut the onions into fine rings and chop the remaining capers, then mix with the balsamic vinegar, the fish sauce, the olive oil and pepper.

Take the salmon out of the bag and divide into large pieces. Mix the salad with the sauce and place the lukewarm salmon on top.

- **Duck breast**

Ingredients for 2 portions
- 2 Duck breast fillet with skin
- 50 g Carrot, diced finely
- 50 g Parsley root, diced finely
- 50 g Shallot, diced finely
- 50 g Apple, diced small
- 50 g Prune, diced finely
- 1 toe Garlic, finely diced
- 20 g Ginger, finely diced

- 100 ml Vegetable broth or broth, unsalted
- 50 ml Soy sauce, dark, naturally brewed
- 3 tbsp. lemon juice
- 1 tsp, heaped Paprika powder, noble sweet
- ½ tsp Pepper, white, finely ground
- Duck fat
- Salt

Preparation

Total time approx. 2 hours 35 minutes

Fry all the small diced ingredients in a greased saucepan, stirring several times. A light roasting set may form. Deglaze with broth, soy sauce and lemon juice and loosen with a wooden spoon. Stir in the peppers and pepper. Now let the sauce simmer lightly for about 10 minutes. Then mix with a hand blender and let cool slightly.

Rinse the duck breast fillets, pat dry with kitchen paper and cut the skin in a diamond shape with a sharp knife. Make sure not to cut into the meat. Fill the fillets with the cooled sauce in a vacuum-proof bag and vacuum.

Now fill a cast iron pot with water, place a thermometer in it and heat the water to 62 ° C on the induction field. When the temperature is reached, insert the sealed bag and close the pot. Now it is important to monitor the temperature of the water for 120 min. It is not a problem on the induction cooker to keep the temperature stable.

After 2 hours remove the bag, pat the meat a little dry, put the sauce in a saucepan and keep warm. Fry the meat in a hot, greased pan on the skin side for 1 min. And on the meat side for 30 - 45 seconds.

Arrange with the sauce and serve with rice, pasta or all kinds of potatoes.

- **Baked onsen egg on spinach**

Ingredients for 2 portions
- 4 Egg, best quality
- 80 g Spinach, frozen
- 10 g Onion, finely diced
- 20 g Carrot
- 50 g North Sea crabs
- 40 g Cream cheese
- 50 g butter
- 50 g Panko
- Salt and pepper
- Nutmeg
- Lemon juice
  Preparation
  Total time approx. 1 hour 10 minutes

An onsen egg is an egg that is cooked in hot Japanese springs, the so-called onsen, at temperatures between 60 and 70 ° C. As a result, the egg yolk cooks, but not the egg white - because that takes at least 72 ° C.

Set the sous vide device to 63 ° C, and when the temperature is reached, cook the eggs in a water bath for 60 minutes at 63 ° C.

In the meantime, finely dice the onions and carrots, you can add other vegetables such as peppers or mushrooms, add the spinach and cook. Season well with salt, pepper and nutmeg.

Mix the crabs with the cream cheese. Possibly readjust the consistency with a small dash of lemon juice, if necessary season with salt and pepper - depending on the taste.

Take the eggs out of the shell, carefully wipe the excess egg white with your finger. Leave out the butter in the pan. Roll the egg yolk in panko and briefly fry until golden on both sides.

Chicken rolls with breadcrumbs

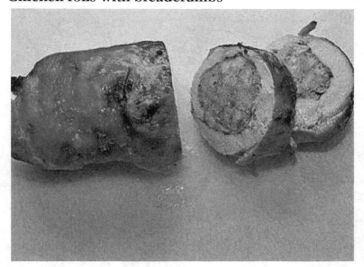

Ingredients for 4 portions

- 4 Chicken breasts, or thighs
- 250 g Bread roll
- 1 Egg
- 100 ml milk
- Salt and pepper
- Herbs, mixed

Preparation

Total time approx. 3 hours 30 minutes

Trigger chicken breasts or thighs and leave the skin as whole as possible.

Make dumplings out of bread cubes, egg, milk and spices. Mix everything and let it steep.

Place the meat flat on cling film, season and top with the dumpling. Form into a roll, put on the skin and wrap with cling film.

Vacuum and cook in a water bath at 68 ° C for about 3 hours.

Remove from the foil and either briefly fry in the preheated oven at 220 ° or flame with the gas burner.

Cut open and serve.

Also cold or warm as a starter or with buffets.

- **Buta no kakuni**

Ingredients for 6 portions
- 1 kg Boneless pork belly
- 100 ml soy sauce
- 100 ml Mirin
- 100 ml sake
- 2 tbsp. fish sauce
- 3 tbsp. sugar
- 3 toes garlic
- 6 cm ginger root
- 3 Spring onions

Preparation

Total time approx. 1 day 12 hours 40 minutes

First cut the pork belly, ideally it should have the same fat and meat layers as possible, cut into approx. 3 cm cubes. The belly can be prepared in the same way with or without a rind.

First place the cubes with the fat side down in a hot pan and fry them vigorously. Since some fat dissolves immediately, no additional fat is needed. Then fry from the other side and remove from the pan.

Mix the mirin, sake, soy sauce, sugar and some fish sauce. Peel and slice garlic and ginger, roughly chop the spring onions.

Vacuum everything together with the pork belly cubes and let it soak in the sous vide cooker at 64 degrees for 36 hours. Of course, it is also much faster if you choose a higher temperature, but then the fat does not transform into a pure, delicate enamel so ideally.

When the cooking time is over, take the meat cubes out of the cooking bags and keep them warm in the oven at 65 ° C. Let the cooking liquid reduce again until it starts to become thick. To serve, cover the pork belly pieces thinly with the very aromatic sauce.

Buta no Kakuni translates from Japanese simply gently cooked pork belly cubes. The variations of this dish consist in particular in the marinade / cooking liquid and the cooking time. Because of the desired slow cooking, the recipe is particularly suitable for the sous vide cooker.

- **Chicken thighs mushrooms**

Ingredients for 2 portions
For the dressing:
- 1 Juice orange, juice thereof, approx. 100 ml
- 50 ml Balsamic vinegar of Modena
- 1 Chili pepper, red
- 2 tbsp. Olive oil, virgin
  For the marinade:
- 70 ml soy sauce
- 10 ml rice vinegar
- Worcestershire sauce, a few drops of it
- 1 tsp. Spice mix (paprika powder, coriander powder, brown sugar)
- 2 toes Garlic, fresher
- 6 Chicken drumstick
- For the salad:
- 75 g Corn salad, cleaned and washed

- 1 Onion, red
- 1 Bell pepper, red
- 1 bunchCoriander, fresher

For the vegetables:

- 400 g Mushrooms, fresh
- 1 tbsp. honey
- 1 tbsp. Almond, chopped
- Clarified butter or oil for frying
- Moreover:
- Salt and pepper

Preparation

Total time approx. 10 hours

For the marinade soy sauce, a good dash of rice vinegar (approx. 10 ml) and a few drops of Worcestershire sauce, mix in a suitable container. Add brown sugar, honey, paprika powder and coriander powder to taste (1 tsp). Finally peel the fresh garlic and press it into the marinade. Mix the chicken drumsticks with the marinade and chill for at least 30 minutes - preferably overnight. There are no limits to the marinade itself. The main thing is that it tastes good.

For the dressing, mix the juice of the freshly squeezed juice orange in a ratio of 2: 1 with balsamic vinegar. Means: 100 ml orange juice on 50 ml balsamic vinegar. Then add a finely chopped chilli pepper and some salt and pepper to the dressing. At the end, whisk the oil into a vinaigrette.

This amount gives dressing for about 4 servings. I like to keep it and then use it the next day.

Wash and clean the lamb's lettuce and mix it with a finely chopped half red onion (depending on the size and taste, of course) and a pepper. Pluck the coriander and mix in as well. Salt and pepper.

Clean the mushrooms, cut them into slices and braise them in a hot pan - preferably in clarified butter, but oil is also possible. Salt and pepper. Add a little honey and sprinkle with the almonds and glaze the mushrooms under the pan.

Drain the chicken well after marinating and vacuum, then cook at 73.9 degrees Celsius for 1 hour. Cut the bag at one corner and pour off the liquid. Spread the thighs on a baking sheet and either crunch them up briefly under the grill or (as I did) flame them with a Bunsen burner.

Brush with a remaining dressing and serve hot next to the lamb's lettuce and mushrooms.

Tip: You can also bake the chicken in the oven.

- **Beetroot carpaccio with oriental duck**

Ingredients for 2 portions
- 2 tuber Beetroot
- 1 pack Feta cheese
- 1 tsp, heaped Dijon mustard
- 1 teaspoon honey
- 1 bunchCoriander, alternatively flat-leaf parsley
- 2 tbsp. Balsamic, lighter

- 2 tbsp. Walnut oil or sesame oil, alternatively olive oil
- 2 tbsp. Cointreau, alternatively orange juice
- Salt and pepper
- 1 handful Pine nuts, alternatively walnut nuts
- 1 tbsp. peppercorns
- 2 Carnation
- 1 teaspoon cinnamon
- 1 teaspoon cardamom powder
- 5 Allspice
- 12 coriander seeds
- ½ tsp chili powder
- ½ tsp paprika
- ½ tsp ginger powder
- 1 duck breast
- Clarified butter

Preparation

Total time approx. 50 minutes

Beetroot in salt water approx. 20 min. cook, let cool and cut into fine slices. Alternatively, use pre-cooked beetroot.

Cut the feta into thin slices. Prepare the plates with beetroot and feta.

For the dressing, mix honey, balsamic vinegar, orange juice, mustard, season with salt and ground pepper.

Roast the remaining spices in the pan without oil, let them cool a bit, and then mortar. Place the seasoning mix in a freezer bag, add the duck breast. Suck the air out of the bag and knot it. Pour boiling water over the bag in a saucepan, 10 min. Let it steep, pour off water and pour boiling water over it again, let it steep again for 10 min.

Roast pine nuts or walnut kernels during this time. Put them on the plates. Roughly chop the coriander or parsley.

Take the duck breast out of the freezer bag and put it in clarified butter or similar. Fry for 4 - 5 min on each side. Put the gravy into the dressing. Let the meat rest a little and cut it as thin as possible. Put the slices on the plates.

Pour the dressing over the carpaccio. Spread the chopped herbs on the plates.

- **The perfect fillet of beef**

Ingredients for 1 portions
- 1 Beef
- 2 Garlic cloves
- 3 Rosemary
- 7 mushrooms
- 2 spring onions
- Oil for frying
- Salt and pepper

Preparation

Total time approx. 2 hours 15 minutes

Unpack the beef fillet and pat it dry, then seal it with the rosemary and peeled garlic in a vacuum bag. Place the bag in the sous vide bath at 53 - 54 ° C. The meat stays here for 2 hours.

Clean the mushrooms and spring onions and cut them into pieces. When the meat comes out of the bath, you can start preparing the side dish so that it still has a bite and is not completely overcooked.

Take the meat out of the bag and grill on the grill using the flip-flip method, i.e. turn every 20 - 30 seconds until a nice crust has formed.

Fry the mushrooms and spring onions for about 5 - 10 minutes in the hot pan and season with just a little pepper and salt.

- **Pulpo salad with salicornes**

Ingredients for 4 portions
- 400 g Squid (Pulp tentacle)
- 5 cl Noilly Prat
- 5 cl Olive oil, mild
- 150 g Queller (Salicornes)
- 12 Cherry tomato
- 30 g pistachios
- 1 Onion, red
- 1 handful salt
- Sea salt, coarse
- For the vinaigrette:
- 4 cl Sherry vinegar
- ½ Garlic cloves
- 8 cl Olive oil, mild

- 1 tsp. Dijon mustard
- Pepper (Tasmanian mountain pepper), freshly ground
- Sugar
- Salt

Preparation

Total time approx. 5 hours 30 minutes

Vacuum the pulp tentacles together with the Noilly Prat and the olive oil and cook in a water bath at 77 ° C for 5 hours. Alternatively, cook the tentacles together with oil and Noilly Prat in a roaster in the oven at around 90 ° C - however, the meat does not gain the same bite-resistant yet tender consistency as with the sous-vide method.

In the meantime, thickly cover the bottom of a baking dish or baking sheet with coarse sea salt, place the halved tomatoes on the salt with the cut surface facing up and dry in the oven at 110 ° C for about 2 hours. The tomatoes should be reduced to about half their volume. Then remove from the oven, let cool and carefully remove salt. The salt can be "forever" reused for similar drying processes.

Blanch the salicornes briefly in boiling water, cool down quickly and pat dry.

Roast the pistachio kernels dry in the oven at about 150 ° C to the desired degree of roasting (never so long that they lose their green color) and let them cool.

Cut the onion into thin rings, mix with a handful of salt and let it steep for an hour. Then rinse carefully and soak in at least one liter of cold water for another hour. Drain the water and carefully pat the onions dry.

Crush the garlic finely and whip with the sherry vinegar, olive oil and mustard into an emulsion. Season well with mountain pepper, sugar and salt. The mountain pepper - which is actually not pepper at all - should clearly taste with its floral, fruity notes.

At the end of the cooking time, take the Pulpo bag out of the water bath and cool down quickly in ice water. Cut the tentacles into rough pieces and serve with the remaining components.

- **Pork tenderloin**

Ingredients for 3 portions
- 500 g Pork fillet (pork roast)
- 750 g Potato
- 750 g Carrot
- Melt butter
- Salt and pepper
- Sugar

Preparation

Total time about 2 hours 30 minutes

Lubricate the meat with melted butter, salt and pepper. Wrap many, many layers of cling film and make sure there is no air under the film. Then knot the ends of the film several times on both sides.

The meat should actually be sealed in with a vacuum device, but those who do not have such a device can use the cling film method. It is important that the meat is absolutely sealed, so it is better to use too much than not enough foil.

Put on a pot of water and heat to exactly 60 ° C. On an electric stove this is between levels 1 and 2 (out of 9). Maintaining exactly this temperature is very important for the result, so plan some time for tempering! Then put the packaged meat in the pot and let it cook for two hours without a lid. Then melt the butter in a very hot cast iron pan for a few seconds and caramelize the meat in it so that a nice brown crust results.

For the French fries rissoles, cut the potatoes into cubes approx. 1 cm long (or use very small and diced baby potatoes) and put them in a pan with cold water. Bring the water to a boil and cook the potatoes for two minutes, then strain.

Melt the butter in a very hot cast iron pan and fry the potatoes until they are nice and brown. Then place the pan with the potatoes in an oven preheated to 180 ° C. Fry the potatoes until they are done.

For the caramelized carrots, cut the carrots crosswise into pieces about 2 cm long and then quarter them. Pour enough water into a coated pan that the bottom is just covered. Add flakes of butter, sugar and carrots. Simmer until brown syrup is made and swirl the carrots in it.

- **Veal roulade with tomato ragout**

Ingredients for 4 portions
1. 8 Roulade, from veal
2. 1 branch rosemary
3. 150 g Tomato, dried, pickled in oil
4. 2 Garlic cloves
5. 50 g Olives, black
6. 100 g Parmesan, in one piece
7. 3 piece Anchovy fillets
8. 2 Tea spoons capers
9. Salt
10. Pepper from the grinder
11. For the ragout:
12. 500 g cherry tomatoes
13. 1 branch rosemary
14. Oregano
15. Basil
16. 4 tbsp.olive oil

Preparation

Total time approx. 1 hour 40 minutes

Preheat a low-temperature cooker (sous vide cooker) to 58 ° C for the roulades. While heating, wash the rosemary, pat dry, pluck the needles and chop finely. Drain the dried tomatoes and peel the garlic. Cut tomatoes, garlic, capers, anchovy fillets and olives into very small cubes and grate the parmesan roughly. For the farce, put all prepared ingredients except the tomatoes in a bowl or in the mortar with a little oil and stir vigorously into a kind of porridge so that all the ingredients are mixed together.

Place the meat slices side by side on a work surface. Brush with the farce, leaving the edges free. Roll up the meat from the narrow side. Either individually, or max. Vacuum 2 roulades in a bag. Cook in the low-temperature oven for 1 hour.

Take out the roulades, season with salt and pepper and sauté very briefly on all sides in a pan.

For the tomato ragout, wash the tomatoes and herbs and shake dry. Pluck the needles or leaves and chop them finely. Put the tomatoes together with the herbs in a vacuum bag and lightly season with salt and pepper. Cook in the low-temperature oven at 85 ° C for 40 minutes.

- **Entrecote with potato gratin**

Ingredients for 2 portions
For the meat:
- 500 g entrecote
- 4 sprig of rosemary
- 4 sprig of thyme
- 2 bay leaves
- 50 g butter

For the gratin:
- 900 g waxy potatoes
- 450 ml whipped cream
- 1 clove of garlic
- 250 g gratin cheese
- 3 pinch of salt, pepper, nutmeg

- 3 shots of white wine

Preparation

Total time approx. 90 minutes

Heat the water bath to the desired temperature. Preheat the oven to 180 ° C (fan oven).

Put the entrecote with rosemary, thyme, bay leaves and the butter in the vacuum bag and mix everything well.

Vacuum bag the meat, put it in the water bath and let it cook for 70 minutes.

Peel, halve and cut the potatoes into thin slices (leave the cut potatoes in their shape, do not pull them apart).

Halve the clove of garlic and rub a baking dish generously.

Place the cut potato halves in the baking dish. When the floor is covered, calmly stack on top of each other. Pour cream and wine over it, season with salt, pepper (potatoes can take a lot of salt) and grate nutmeg over it. Sprinkle cheese over the potato-cream mixture and slide the baking dish into the preheated oven for 60 minutes.

Heat the pan to the highest setting, if it starts to smoke, add butter and the steak and roast briefly on all sides until a uniform crust forms. Preheat the device on the highest flame for preparation in the beefer. Adjust the insert so that the meat is 1 cm away from the burner. Put the grate in the meat and depending on the thickness, steak the steak for 15-30 seconds on each side.

Put the meat on a preheated plate, salt and serve with the gratin.

- **Fruit salad with zabaione**

Ingredients for 2 portions
For the salad:

- 2 pears
- 1 baby pineapple
- 10 strawberries
- 10 dark table grapes
- 2 kiwi
- 4 sprig of rosemary
- 4 sprig thyme
- 1 handful of fresh mint
- 3 teaspoons of brown cane sugar

- 4 tablespoons of rum
- 1 teaspoon of salt

For the Zabaione:

- 4 egg yolks
- 4 teaspoons of sugar
- 100 ml white wine
- 1 shot of amaretto (optional)

Preparation

Total time approx. 150 minutes

Preheat the water bath to 60 ° C.

Cut the pears lengthwise into eighths, remove the core, lightly sprinkle with salt and divide the rosemary sprigs into two bags.

Cut the peel of the pineapple, quarter the fruit lengthways and cut out the stalk. Sprinkle with brown sugar, put in a bag, add mint leaves and refine with rum.

Wash off the strawberries and pat dry. Halve lengthways and divide into two bags.

Wash the grapes, dry them, halve them lengthways and put them in a foil bag.

Peel and quarter the kiwi and place in a bag with the sprigs of thyme.

Cook the strawberries for 15 minutes. Then remove the bag from the water and let it cool in a bowl with cold water.

Heat the water bath to 65 ° C. Add the kiwi and grapes to the water and, if necessary, attach the bag to the pot with the clothes pegs. Cook for 15 minutes. Remove the bag and place in the cool water basin with the strawberries.

Heat the water bath to 75 ° C. add the pears and cook for 30 minutes. Remove the bag and put it in cold water.

Heat the water bath to 85 ° C. Add the bag of pineapple and cook for 90 minutes. Put in cold water.

Cut open the foil bag, remove the herbs and arrange the fruit on plates.

Prepare the zabaione just before serving. To do this, separate the eggs and put the yolks in the metal bowl. Add sugar, wine and amaretto and beat the mixture over a boiling water bath for about 1 minute until the consistency is creamy. Serve with fruit salad.

- **Sous vide carrot**

Ingredients for 2 portions

- 6 medium sized carrots
- 3 pinch of salt
- 2 teaspoons of powdered sugar
- 2 shots of olive oil

Preparation

Total time approx. 40 minutes

Heat the water bath to 75 ° C.

Peel the carrots and cut lengthways in the middle.

Place in a foil bag, pour the oil and icing sugar over it and mix well in the bag.

Vacuum the carrots and put them in a tempered water bath for 35 minutes.

After cooking, take the carrots out of the water bath and heat a grill pan at the highest setting until steam rises. Put the carrots in, press lightly and fry for approx. 2 minutes until you can see a nice roasted pattern.

- **Crispy chicken breasts with salad**

Ingredients for 2 portions
For the meat:
- 1 whole chicken breast (with skin)
- 50 g butter
- 1 teaspoon of salt, pepper
- Rapeseed or sunflower oil (for frying)
For the salad:
- 2 large lettuce hearts (romaine lettuce)
For the dressing
- 3 anchovies (from the glass)
- 1 clove of garlic
- 5 dashes of lemon juice

- 250 g crème fraiche
- 3 tablespoons of olive oil
- 150 g parmesan
- 3 pinch of black pepper
  For the bread slices (crostini)
- 4 slices of ciabatta
- 4 teaspoons of olive oil
- 1 clove of garlic

Preparation

Total time approx. 60 minutes

Preheat the water bath to 60 ° C with a sous vide stick.

Salt, pepper and put the chicken breast in the foil bag. Add butter. Seal the bag, put it in a water bath, fix it to the pan and cook for 60 minutes.

For the dressing, add garlic, anchovies, oil, crème fraiche and the lemon juice to a mortar and pound everything thoroughly until a paste is formed (alternatively, of course, you can also use a hand blender or a food processor). Season with pepper and lemon juice. Salt is not needed because the anchovies give enough seasoning.

Cut the lettuce into thin strips and wash them thoroughly in a colander under cold water.

When the cooking time for the chicken breast has expired, place the grill pan on the stove and heat to the highest setting.

Take the foil bag out of the water bath, take out the meat and pat dry with kitchen paper. When the pan is steaming, add a small dash of rapeseed or sunflower oil and place the poultry in the pan, skin side down. Gently pressing the grill strips on the jumps.

Drizzle ciabatta slices on both sides with olive oil. Put in the pan and fry briefly on both sides.

Add the dressing to the salad and fold in. Cut open the chicken breast and place on the salad. Pour parmesan over the salad. Rub the crostini with half a clove of garlic and serve with the salad.

- **Fillet of beef on mashed potatoes**

Ingredients for 3 portions
For the meat:

- 350 g beef fillet
- 30 g butter
- 2 sprig of rosemary
- 2 sprig of thyme
- 1 clove of garlic, cut into thin slices
- Salt

For the pounding:

- 300 g floury potatoes
- 200 g sweet potatoes
- 150 ml whipped cream
- 100 g butter
- 3 sprig of fresh marjoram
- 3 sprig of fresh coriander

- Salt, pepper, nutmeg
  For the reduction:
- 400 ml red wine
- 100 ml beef stock
- 5 sprig of fresh rosemary
- 5 sprig of fresh thyme
- 1 bulb of garlic
- Salt pepper
- 50 g butter
- 1 teaspoon of tomato paste
- 2 tablespoons of starch (dissolved in twice the amount of water)
- 30 g sugar
- 2 tablespoons of olive oil

Preparation

Total time approx. 90 minutes

Preheat the water bath to 54 ° C.

Pat the fillet dry with kitchen paper and add to the foil bag with rosemary, thyme, garlic slices and butter. Massage ingredients from the outside into the bag so that everything mixes well.

Vacuum the meat, put it in a water bath and cook for 90 minutes. Slice the whole garlic bulb lengthways and place it cut side down in a saucepan.

Lightly roast the garlic, first add olive oil, then butter, the fresh herbs and tomato paste and sauté everything vigorously for 1 minute.

Deglaze with wine, pour on the stock and simmer on a medium heat for about 40 minutes until the reduction has a creamy consistency, stirring occasionally.

Peel and quarter the potatoes for the mash. Place in a pan of cold water and cook over medium heat until soft (about 25 minutes).

Pass the sauce through a sieve. Set the Hotplate to the highest level, add the sugar and starch to the sauce and let everything boil up once. Reduce to medium heat and simmer for 20 minutes until a creamy consistency is achieved.

Add the cream, butter and the chopped herbs to the potatoes and mash everything briefly. Season with salt, pepper and nutmeg.

Remove the vacuum bag with the meat from the water bath and hold briefly under cold water. Heat the pan to the highest level. Pat the meat dry, salt and briefly roast from both sides until a crispy crust has formed.

- **Hollandaise sauce**

Ingredients for 2 portions

- 150 g butter
- 2 egg yolks
- 60 ml water

- 10 ml white wine vinegar
- 3 g salt

Preparation

Total time approx. 30 minutes

Fill the tub of the sous vide cooker with water and heat to 75 ° C.

Melt the butter and fill it with the egg yolk, water, lemon juice, white wine vinegar and salt in a vacuum bag.

Place the bag on the vacuum sealer and switch it on. Keep a close eye on the egg mass: only a little air needs to be sucked out of the bag. If too much liquid is sucked in, it spills into the vacuum sealer. Then seal the bag.

Place the bag in the sous vide cooker and let it rest for 30 minutes in a water bath.

Cut the bag and fill the mass into the siphon. Screw the siphon on, insert the N2O cartridges and shake vigorously. Spray the hollandaise sauce from the siphon onto the plates.

- **Pulled pork - sous vide cooked**

Ingredients for 4 portions
For the spice mix:
- 1 tablespoon of paprika powder
- 1 tablespoon of brown sugar
- 1 teaspoon of salt
- 3 mustard seeds
- 1 pinch of black pepper
- 2 pinch of garlic powder
- 1 pinch of oregano
- 1/2 teaspoon of coriander seeds
- 1 pinch of chili flakes
  For the pulled pork

- 700 g pork shoulder
Spice mix:
- 500 g of French fries
- Bbq sauce
- 3 spring onions

Preparation

Total time approx. 15 hour

For the spice mix, mix all the ingredients together thoroughly.

Fill sous vide cooker with water and heat to 74 ° C. Rub in meat with half of the spice mixture from all sides. Place in a vacuum bag and vacuum.

Put the meat in the water bath and let it cook for about 16 hours.

Preheat the oven to 150 ° C. Remove the meat from the vacuum bag and carefully pat dry with kitchen paper. Rub in with the rest of the spice mixture. Cook in the oven for about 3 hours. As soon as the roast thermometer shows 92 ° C, remove the roast and let it rest for another 20 minutes.

Fry the french fries according to the package instructions, degrease them on kitchen paper and season with salt and paprika powder.

Put the meat on a board. Cut into bite-size pieces with 2 large forks. Add BBQ sauce and mix until everything is well wetted with sauce. Season with salt. Cut the spring onions into rings.

Serve the pulled pork with french fries, spring onions and BBQ sauce.

- **Salmon with carrots and pea mash**

Ingredients for 4 portions
For the salmon:
- 350 g salmon fillet (with skin)
- 1 piece of ginger (approx. 5 cm each)
- 2 tablespoons of olive oil
- For the carrots
- 6 medium sized carrots
- 3 pinch of salt
- 2 teaspoons of powdered sugar
- 3 tablespoons of olive oil
  For the peas
- 250 g peas (freezer)
- 100 ml fish stock (or vegetable stock)
- 2 shots of white wine
- 1 clove of garlic
- 1/2 red onion
- 1 dash of olive oil

- 2 sprinkles of lime juice
- 1 lime (the zest)
- 1 handful of fresh coriander
- 1 handful of fresh mint
- Salt pepper

Preparation

Total time approx. 175 minutes

Preheat the water bath to 83 ° C.

Peel the carrots and cut in half lengthways. Put in a foil bag with a little olive oil, salt and powdered sugar and vacuum.

Place in a tempered water bath and cook for 2 hours.

Cut the ginger into thin slices for the fish (does not need to be peeled), pat the salmon dry, rub with olive oil and salt. Vacuum everything together in a foil bag and put in the fridge.

Finely dice the onion and garlic for the pea mash, grate the peel from the lime and roughly chop the herbs.

Heat some olive oil in a saucepan. Braise the onions and garlic until translucent over a medium heat for about 4 minutes. Deglaze with the stock and white wine and simmer for 10 minutes on low heat.

At the end of the cooking time, take the carrots out of the water, put them aside and adjust the water bath to 55 ° C by adding cold water

Take the salmon out of the fridge and put them in a water bath for 45 minutes.

Remove the saucepan with the stock from the stove, add the frozen peas and close the lid (the peas only need to thaw. If you cook in the pot for too long, they quickly lose their color and turn brownish-gray).

Set the hob to the highest setting and place the cast iron pan on it.

The pan starts to smoke, take the salmon out of the bag, remove the ginger and fry the fish until crispy in the hot pan on the side of the skin. Take the carrots out of the bag and sauté well next to the

60

fish. For the characteristic grill pattern, turn the salmon 90 degrees after 45 seconds.

Add herbs, lime juice and zest, butter, salt and pepper to the peas and roughly crush them with a hand blender.

Put the pea mash in the middle of a plate, top with the salmon and arrange carrots next to it.

- **Green asparagus**

Ingredients for 4 portions
- 450 g asparagus
- 2 pinch of paprika powder
- 1/2 tablespoon of garlic flakes
- 1 teaspoon of coarse sea salt
- 2 tablespoons of butter
- 1 lime

Preparation

Total time approx. 60 minutes

Fill sous vide cooker with water and bring it to 57 ° C.

Cut the lime into wedges. Approximately Cut away 1-2 cm of the asparagus ends and peel the lower third. Put the asparagus with the remaining ingredients in a vacuum bag and vacuum.

Put the asparagus in the water bath and cook for 1 hour. Cut the bag open and serve as an accompaniment to, for example, beef fillet or chicken breast.

- **Poached egg with pancakes**

Ingredients for 4 portions

For the vegetable pancakes:

- 130 g flour
- 1/2 teaspoon of baking soda

- 2 pinch of black pepper
- 1 pinch of cayenne pepper
- 60 g cauliflower
- 60 g broccoli
- 1/2 bunch of parsley
- 2 spring onions
- 100 g cheddar
- 1 egg
- 230 ml milk
- 2 tablespoons of olive oil
- Salt

  For the poached eggs
- 4 eggs

Preparation

Total time approx. 45 minutes

Fill sous vide cooker with water and preheat to 75 ° C. Add eggs and cook for 16 minutes.

Mix the flour with baking soda, salt, black pepper and cayenne pepper.

Cut the spring onions into rings. Finely chop the cauliflower, broccoli and parsley. Mix with the spring onions, egg, milk and cheddar cheese. Gradually add the flour mixture.

Heat olive oil in a pan. Put 1-2 ladles of dough in the pan and spread lightly. Bake pancakes on medium heat until golden brown from the bottom. Turnover and drain on kitchen paper. Do the same with the rest of the dough.

Spread the vegetable pancakes on a plate. Remove the eggs from the sous vide cooker and beat them carefully. Slide the poached eggs onto the pancakes and serve.

- **Asparagus sous vide**

Ingredients for 4 servings
- 500 g Asparagus, white
- 0.5 tsp. sugar
- 0.5 tsp.salt
- 1 stk. Lemon the peel of it
- 30 g butter

Preparation

Total time approx. 35minutes

Peel the white asparagus and remove the woody end and place in the vacuum bag.

Grate the peel of the untreated organic lemon with a grater and add it to the bag along with the butter, sugar and salt.

Now remove the air from the bag using a vacuum device and seal the bag.

The sealed bag is now placed in the steam cooker or in a sous vide device for approx. 30 minutes at 85 degrees.

Take the finished asparagus out of the bag and serve with boiled potatoes and a hollandaise sauce.

- **Sous-vide spare ribs**

Ingredients for 2 portions
- 2 kg Spareribs

Ingredients for the marinade
- 1 tsp. paprika
- 1 tsp. Cumin, ground
- 1 tsp. Chili powder or chili salt
- 1 tsp. oregano
- 1 black pepper, ground
- 1 salt
- 1 tsp. garlic powder
- 1 shot lemon juice
- 5 tbsp. Barbecue Sauce

Preparation
Total time approx. 315 minutes

For the sous vide spare ribs, first make a hearty marinade. Mix the paprika powder, cumin, chili powder, oregano, pepper, salt, garlic powder and lemon juice with the barbecue sauce in a bowl.

Rub the spare ribs well with this marinade and place the ribs lying down, side by side in the vacuum bag and vacuum.

Now cook the spare ribs for a good 5 hours at 80 degrees in a sous-vide device or in a steam cooker.

Then rinse the spare ribs immediately with cold water, take the meat out of the bag and put it on the hot grill - for about 8-12 minutes. If you want, you can coat the spare ribs with a little barbecue sauce after grilling - but this is not necessary.

- **Sous vide carrot sticks**

Ingredients for 4 portions
- 400 g carrots
- 1 tbsp. butter
- 1 tsp. Ginger, grated
- 1 tsp. Fennel seeds, whole

Preparation

Total time approx. 65 minutes

Wash the carrots, clean them, peel them with a potato peeler and cut them into elongated sticks.

Now put the carrot sticks side by side in a vacuum bag. Put the grated ginger and the fennel seeds in the bag with the carrots and vacuum them.

Now put the bag in the sous vide device or in the steam cooker and cook for 60 minutes at 80 degrees.

Then quench the bag in ice water (or cold water), remove the carrots from the bag and swirl them briefly in a little butter in a pan.

- **Pork fillet from the sous vide**

Ingredients for 4 portions
- 600 g Pork loin / Pork
- 1 shot Oil for the pan
- 1 salt
- 1 pepper

100 min. Total time
Preparation
Total time approx. 100 minutes
For the pork fillet using the sous-vide process, wash the meat first and pat dry with the kitchen towel.
Now use a sharp knife to remove any fat residues and the silver skin from the meat and cut into slices of any size (approx. 3-4 cm) thick - of course you can also cook the whole piece.

Now the pieces of meat come into the vacuum bag and the air is sucked out and welded with the help of a vacuum device.

The welded-in bag is then placed in the steamer or in a sous-vide device for approx. 60 minutes at 63 degrees (= medium) or 67 degrees.

After gentle cooking, take the bag out again, cut it open with a knife or scissors, dry the meat a little with kitchen paper and season it with salt and pepper.

Finally, a dash of oil is heated in a pan and the meat is spicy on all sides and only briefly seared - important, the oil must be very hot.

- **Mashed potatoes sous vide**

Ingredients for 4 portions

- 1 kg Potatoes, cooked with flour
- 250 ml milk
- 30 g butter
- Salt
- Nutmeg

Preparation

Total time approx. 100 minutes

For the mashed potatoes, wash and peel the potatoes first. Then vacuum and seal the potatoes in a vacuum bag.

The bag of potatoes is placed in the steam cooker or sous vide device for 90 minutes at 85 degrees.

Then take the potatoes out of the bag and mash them in a saucepan and heat them up on a low setting.

Heat the milk together with the butter in another bowl and stir into the potato mixture with a whisk. Season the mashed potatoes with salt and a pinch of nutmeg.

- **Hokkaido pumpkin sous vide**

Ingredients for 2 portions

- 1 stk Hokkaido pumpkin (400 grams of it)
- Salt
- Pepper
- 1 tsp. butter
- 1 tsp. Butter for the pan
- Ginger, grated
- 1 shot Apple juice

Preparation

Total time approx. 25 minutes

Wash the Hokkaido pumpkin well, cut it in half and use a spoon to remove the pulp with the seeds - do not throw it away, the seeds can be dried and used to decorate various dishes.

Now cut the pumpkin (including the skin) into bite-size cubes and add it together with the ginger, butter, salt, pepper and a dash of apple juice to the vacuum bag and vacuum it - make sure that no liquid gets onto the weld seam of the bag.

72

Now cook the pumpkin pieces in a bag at 80 degrees for 20 minutes in a sous vide or steam cooker.

After the cooking process, remove the bag, open it and briefly fry the pumpkin pieces in a pan with a little butter.

- **Pork medallions from sous vide**

Ingredients for 4 servings

- 800 g pork filets
- Salt
- Pepper
- Oil for the pan

Preparation

Total time approx. 75 minutes

For the pork medallions from sous vide, first wash the meat, pat dry and cut into slices of approx. 3-4 cm.

Now season the pieces of meat with salt and pepper, put them in a vacuum bag and remove the air with the help of the vacuum device and seal the bag.

The bag at 63 degrees for about 60 minutes in the steam cooker or in the sous-vide device.

Then cut the bag open, take out the meat and sear in a pan with oil on all sides - the oil should be very hot and the meat should be seared only very briefly.

- **Salmon sous vide**

Ingredients for 4 portions
- 4 stk Salmon fillet, without skin
- Sea-salt
- Peppercorns, black
- 1 shot lemon juice
- 2 stk Dill stalks, chopped
- 2 stk Sprig of thyme, chopped
- 2 tbsp. olive oil

Preparation

Total time approx. 40 minutes

First wash off the salmon fillets (approx. 180 grams each - 3 cm thick), pat dry with kitchen paper and remove any bones.

Now make a marinade from olive oil, the cut dill stalks, salt, pepper, lemon juice and the cut thyme sprigs and rub the fish fillets with it.

Then put the fillets (including the marinade) in a vacuum bag - do not lay them next to each other - vacuum and cook the bags for 30 minutes at 52 degrees in a sous vide device or in a steam cooker. After the cooking process, remove the fish fillets from the bag and serve - a side dish is a potato gratin or boiled potatoes.

- **Duck breast in orange sauce**

Ingredients for 4 portions
- 4 stk duck breast
- 1 prize salt
- 1 tbsp. Butter for the pan
- Ingredients for the orange sauce
- 1 orange
- 1 clove of garlic
- 1 tbsp. Butter for the pan
- 1 prize salt

Preparation
Total time approx. 40 minutes

Wash the duck breast pieces of meat and pat them dry. Then free the meat of unwanted tendons, skin and fat (these pieces can be used for a soup) and cut crosswise on the skin side.

Now place the pieces of meat side by side in the vacuum bag and vacuum seal the bag.

Cook the bag at 66 degrees (= medium) or 72 degrees (= through) for 35 minutes.

Then take the meat out of the bag (catch the cooking juice) and fry in a hot pan with butter on both sides - a little longer on the skin side.

Open the orange for the orange sauce and remove the pulp from the skin. Cut the orange pieces into small pieces - catch the juice and sweat together with the orange pieces and the garlic clove in a pan with a little butter.

Now mix the cooking juice from the vacuum bag and let it boil briefly - season with a pinch of salt.

- **Apple millefeuille with berry sauce**

Ingredients for 4 portions
- 300 g puff pastry
- 300 g berries
- 60 g cane sugar
- 1 small bunch of mint
- 50 milliliters of rum
- 500 g Golden Delicious apples
- 70 g granulated sugar
- 50 g pine nuts
- 50 g sultanas
- 1 vanilla pod
- 50 g powdered sugar

Preparation

Total time approx. 3 hour 5 minutes

Fill the water bath and pre-heat it to 65 ° C.

Mix ¾ of the berries with the cane sugar, add half of the mint and the rum and put it all together in a vacuum bag, seal well and cook for 15 minutes 65 ° C. Allow to cool, mix well and strain.

Now refill a water bath and preheat it to 60 ° C.

Peel the apples and remove the core, cut into segments and put them in a vacuum bag together with the crystal sugar, pine nuts, raisins and vanilla. Close the bag tightly and immerse it completely in a sous vide water bath and then cook it for 12 minutes at 60 ° C. Let cool well.

Roll out the puff pastry and cut 10 cm slices of it. Then place it on a baking sheet and bake it at 180 ° C for 6 minutes in the oven.

After baking, cut the puff pastry slices in half, fill them with the apple and place on the serving dishes. Sprinkle last with some berry sauce and the remaining mint.

- **Apple millefeuille with mousse**

Ingredients for 4 portions
Sous vide apple:
- 400 g Golden Delicious apples
- 80 g granulated sugar
- 1 vanilla pod
- Sous vide mousse:
- 3 deciliters of milk
- 3 deciliters of cream
- 1 cinnamon stick
- 6 egg yolks
- 90 grams of granulated sugar
Puff pastry:
- 400 g puff pastry
- Garnish:
- Pine nuts

- Raisins

Preparation

Total time approx. 27 minutes

Sous vide apple:

Peel the apples and remove the core, then cut them into segments and put them in a sous vide vacuum bag together with the granulated sugar and the vanilla. When the bag is properly closed, fully immerse it in the water bath and cook for 12 minutes at 60 ° C sous vide until done.

Then let it cool well.

Sous vide mousse:

Beat the egg yolks with the sugar well and add the cream and the milk. Put this mixture together with the cinnamon in a vacuum bag. Seal the bag well and immerse it in the sous vide water bath.

Then let it cook for 15 minutes on 92 ° C sous vide.

Then allow the mixture to cool. Pass it through a sieve and pour the cream into a siphon with a gas cartridge. Keep it in the fridge.

Puff pastry:

Roll out the puff pastry and cut 10 cm slices of it. Then place it on a baking sheet and bake it at 190 ° C for 20 minutes in the oven.

Garnish:

Place the puff pastry on the serving dishes; add the apples and finish with the cinnamon cream, pine nuts and raisins.

- **Sous vide salmon with dill**

Ingredients for 4 portions
Sous vide salmon:
- 400 grams of salmon fillet without bones and skin
- 40 milliliters of rapeseed oil or sunflower oil
- The zest of 1 lemon
- Salt
Cucumber:
- 2 cucumbers
- 1 small bunch of dill
- The zest and juice of 1 lime
- 2 tablespoons rapeseed oil
- Salt
- Sugar
Preparation
Total time approx. 18 minutes
Sous vide salmon:
Cut the salmon into four equal pieces and vacuum together with the other ingredients in a vacuum bag.

Cook the salmon pieces for 18 minutes at 56 ° C in a sous vide water bath, add salt to taste and place each piece on a plate with the cucumber salad.

Cucumber:

Peel the cucumbers, cut them in half and cut into sickle-shaped slices. Put this together with the salt, the sugar and the lemon zest in a vacuum bag and vacuum. Marinate in the fridge for 2 hours.

Finely chop the dill and make a vinaigrette of the lime juice and the oil.

Marinate the cucumbers with the vinaigrette and season with dill.

- **Beef roulade with onion sauce**

Ingredients for 1 portion
- 4 slices of beef, for example the lid of the topside is very suitable for roulade.
- 4 tablespoons medium-sized mustard
- 2 large pickles
- 1 tablespoon bacon
- 1 medium-sized onion, finely chopped
- 1 teaspoon of fresh marjoram leaves
- A little balsamic vinegar
- Salt
- 300 milliliters of gravy

Preparation
Total time approx. 2 hour
Flatten the roulade slices, brush with mustard and sprinkle with some salt.
Put the bacon cubes in a pan and fry them together with the onions.

84

Stir in the marjoram leaves and lightly acidify the whole with some vinegar.

Allow this mixture to cool and place it at the bottom of the roulade.

Slice the pickles and place them on the onions. Fold the sides in a little and roll up firmly.

Vacuum the portions together with the gravy and cook it for 2 hours at 65 ° C in a sous vide water bath.

Remove the roulade from the bag and serve with the sauce. Tie the sauce if necessary.

- **Sous vide infused mojito**

Ingredients for 2 portions
- 750 ml of rum
- 4 medium-sized stems of lemongrass - lightly bruised (use of kitchen hammer)
- 4 kaffir lime leaves
- Peel of 1 lime
- Juice of 1 lime
- 3 medium-sized sprigs of fresh mint leaves
- Sparkling water

Preparation
Total time approx. 4 hour
Pre-heat your sous vide water bath to 57 ° C.
Place all ingredients in a vacuum bag and close completely by removing as much air as possible. Immerse in a sous vide water bath and cook for 4 hours.
Remove from water and cool completely. Best if refrigerated.

86

- **Sous vide tenderloin**

Ingredients for 4 portions
- 500 grams of tenderloin from New Zealand
- 3 tablespoons peanut oil
- 1 teaspoon of olive oil, extra virgin
- 750 milliliters of red wine
- 3 bottles of port
- 750 milliliters of meat stock
- 200 grams of goose liver
- 200 grams of chicken liver
- Salt and pepper
- 100 grams of peas, fresh or frozen
- 50 milliliter veal stock
- 1 carrot
- 50 grams of black truffle
- 50 milliliters of champagne

- 150 grams of pearl onions
- 5 juniper berries

Preparation method

Total time approx. 60 minutes

Pour 750ml of red wine, the port and the meat stock into a pan in which you can make sauce and let it simmer until it has a syrupy texture.

Prepare the liver cream by sautéing the foie gras and the chicken liver separately. Do not keep the fat. Season with salt and pepper and cut into cubes.

Boil the stock from 750 ml to about 100 ml and then add the diced liver. Puree the mixture and sieve it through a fine sieve to make a fine, soft cream.

Prepare the pea puree by briefly blanching the fresh peas in boiling salt water; if you use frozen peas, let them thaw first. Puree the peas with the veal stock and season with salt and pepper.

Cut the carrot into thin strips with a peeler. Blanch them briefly in boiling salt water and scare them in ice water. Make small rolls of it and place it on a plate. Place in the oven at a low temperature to keep them warm.

Cook the truffles for about an hour in a sealed pan in 50ml champagne and 50ml port. Then remove them from the brew and cut into small dice.

Peel the pearl onion and fry in a pan with a little peanut oil. Deglaze with 500ml port, add three juniper berries and let it boil for about 5 minutes. Let it cook for another 20 minutes with the lid on the pan.

Salt the tenderloin lightly and brush with the olive oil. Vacuum the meat together with two juniper berries in a vacuum bag. Place the meat in a sous vide water bath at 60 ° C for 1 hour.

Then remove the meat from the bag, pat it dry and briefly fry it in a pan with a little peanut oil on both sides at high temperature. Mix the meat juice with the marinated pearl onions.

Cut the beef fillet diagonally and divide it into four plates. Add a scoop of pea puree and liver cream. Arrange the carrot rolls and the pearl onions on the plate. Pour the sauce around the entire dish and enjoy!

- **Sous vide romanesco broccoli**

Ingredients for 4 portions

- 700 grams of Romanesco broccoli (about 450 grams left when cleaned)
- 20 grams cubed salted butter
- 1 pinch of nutmeg

Preparation method

Total time approx. 60 minutes

Cut Romanesco broccoli into small florets, clean them, wash them thoroughly and dry them well. Blanch them briefly in salted water and then scare them in ice water.

Place the vegetables next to each other in a boil-proof bag, sprinkle the nutmeg over it, add the salted butter and distribute everything well over the Romanesco broccoli.

Vacuum and cook the vegetables for 60 minutes at 80 ° C in the sous vide water bath.

Then scare it in ice water. To serve, heat the broccoli again in the bag and then lightly fry the florets in a pan.

- **Vegetarian celeriac burgers**

Ingredients for 1 portion
- 4 Sous Vide celeriac slices
- 1 red onion
- 1 beef tomato
- 4 slices of cheddar cheese
- 4 (hamburger) sandwiches
- 2 pickles
- Tomato Salsa
- 100 grams of iceberg lettuce
- Curry mayonnaise (from 100 ml mayonnaise, 1 tsp curry powder and 1 tsp ginger syrup)

Preparation
Total time approx. 15 minutes
Grill the celeriac slices for 4 minutes per side in the grill pan
Preheat the oven to 180 ° C
Cut the red onion into rings and slice the tomato.
Place the celeriac slices on a baking sheet and place a slice of tomato on each slice
Put a few red onion rings on top and a slice of cheddar cheese. Place in the preheated oven for 3 minutes.

Cut the rolls in half and grill them briefly in the grill pan or on the grill plate. Cover the halves with tomato salsa

Remove the celeriac burgers from the oven and place them on the lower halves of bread. Cut the pickle into long slices and place a slice on top of each burger.

Mix the curry mayonnaise with the finely chopped iceberg lettuce and scoop this on top of the burgers. Cover with the rest of the bread halves.

- **Infused pineapple**

Ingredients for 1 portion
1. ½ pineapple
2. Knob of butter
3. 1 cinnamon stick
4. ¼ vanilla bean
5. 4 cardamom pods
6. 2 star anise
7. Dash of brown rum

Preparation

Clean the pineapple by cutting off the skin and cutting out the hard core.

Cut into thick slices and put in a vacuum bag.

Place the spices and the knob of butter on top and add a dash of brown rum.

Vacuum the pineapple.

Place the sous-video stick on a pan of water and set at 82.5 ° C and add the pineapple when the water is up to temperature.

Let the pineapple cook for 5 minutes.

Take out of the bag and serve immediately at your own discretion whereby the 'rum butter' can absolutely be spooned over the pineapple or immediately cool the pineapple back in ice water and save for a later moment.

- **Veal cheek with cabbage**

Ingredients for 4 portions

- 4 veal cheeks
- Oriental rub
- Fresh (lemon) thyme
- Rosemary & sage
- 8 cloves of garlic (crushed)
- Clarified butter or goose fat
- White pepper (freshly ground)
- Flour, 8 new potatoes (scrubbed and halved)
- 1 small green cabbage
- ½ bag of pre-cooked chestnuts
- 1 tsp caraway seed (crushed)
- 1 bottle of wheat beer
- 125 ml vegetable or chicken broth
- Cranberry compote (jar)

Preparation

Brush the four veal cheeks with olive oil, coat them with the oriental rub and sprinkle with some freshly ground pepper and salt.

Put each veal cheek in its own vacuum bag with fresh thyme, sage, rosemary, crushed garlic and a generous dash of mild olive oil. Vacuum the meat.

Heat the sous-vide cooker to 80 ° C. When the device has reached the correct temperature, place the vacuum bags in the holder. Note: the bags must hang under water.

Remove the bags from the cooker after 6 to 8 hours (depending on the thickness of the meat after vacuuming) and immediately cool them back in ice water.

Remove the meat from the bags and remove the herbs and garlic. Cut the veal cheeks into 3 pieces each. Sprinkle the meat with freshly ground white pepper and salt. Lightly fold the meat on both sides through the flour.

Sear the meat all over high heat in some clarified butter or goose fat and roast until crispy in about 4 minutes. Let the meat rest in a warm place.

Boil the new potatoes for about 10 minutes in water with a little salt.

Meanwhile, cut the cabbage in half and tear the leaves into pieces. Bake the chestnuts for 5 minutes over medium heat in some butter. Add the caraway seed and the cabbage. Scoop a few times. Deglaze the chestnuts with the white beer and add the stock. Bring the whole to the boil and then lower the heat completely. Cook the cabbage with a lid on the pan in about 7 minutes.

Brown the potatoes in some butter for about 5 minutes.

Carve the meat. Divide the cabbage over 4 pre-heated deep plates, place the veal cheek slices on top of it and spread the chestnuts and new potatoes over it. Spoon some cranberry compote over the dish here and there.

- **Tournedos rossini**

Ingredients for 2 portions
Duck liver:
- 200 g of duck liver
- 1/2 cocktail glass vieux
- Powdered sugar

Tenderloin and gravy:
- 4 pieces of tenderloin
- (120/140 g) oil and butter
- 1 dl Madeira
- 75 g truffle tapenade
- 3 dl veal stock

Brioche bread:
- 4 thick slices of brioche bread (2 cm)
- 1 clove of garlic
- Oil

Potatoes and asparagus:
- 500 g young potatoes, in the skin
- 12 green asparagus

Preparation
Preparation of duck liver:

Allow the duck liver to warm up and remove veins and blood vessels.

Put the duck liver in a large container. Add the vieux and mix well. Season with pepper, salt and a pinch of powdered sugar (make sure it doesn't get too sweet).

Pour this into a suitable baking tin and let it set in the fridge for about 2 hours.

Preparation Tenderloin and gravy:

Fry the tenderloin briefly in hot oil. Then let cool slightly from the pan.

Vacuum the meat.

Let the meat cook sous vide for 4 hours at 56 °C.

Deglaze the broth with the Madeira, truffle tapenade and veal stock.

Reduce this to 1/3 and season to taste.

Preparation of brioche bread:

Cut the brioche bread into large slices.

Chop the garlic and vegetables very briefly in oil.

Coat the bread with the garlic oil and make it crispy in the oven at 180°C.

Preparation of potatoes and asparagus:

Wash the potatoes well. Cut them in half, cook until al dente and let cool.

Blanch the asparagus in boiling water with salt and cool them back in ice water.

- **Scalloped gratin**

Ingredients
- 800 grams of salsify
- 2 tbsp. panko
- 2 tbsp. pine nuts
- 4 sprigs of lemon thyme
- 50 grams of pecorino cheese

Preparation method

Preheat the oven with grill setting to 190 ° C.

Arrange the salsify tightly next to each other in a greased baking dish or on a greased baking tray.

Remove the lemon thyme from the twigs and sprinkle with the salsify.

Season generously with freshly ground pepper and some salt and sprinkle with pine nuts and panko.

Grate the pecorino cheese over it and grease in the preheated oven until the panko is nicely crispy and the cheese is colored and melted.

- **Chicken with broccoli cheese sauce**

Ingredients for 4 portions
- 4 Chicken fillet
- 1 Broccoli
- 3 shallots
- 10pieces Mushroom
- 40 g butter
- 5 g salt
- 2 cloves garlic
- 100 g white wine
- 350 grams of whipped cream
- 100 grams of Gouda Cheese

Preparation

Total time approx. 1 hour 30 minutes

Heat the sous vide bath to 65 degrees. Put the chicken fillet in a vacuum bag with a generous dash of olive oil and a pinch of salt. Once the water bath is up to temperature, put the chicken in and set the timer to 1 hour.

Cut the florets off the broccoli and cut the broccoli stem into small pieces. Cut the shallot into pieces and grind it with the broccoli stem in a food processor.

Clean the mushrooms (if necessary) and cut into quarters.

Melt the butter in a pan. Add salt, finely chopped garlic and the broccoli onion mix and fry for 5 minutes. Add the wine and let it reduce until there is almost no moisture left in the pan. Then add the whipped cream and cheese and stir well until a fondue-like structure is created.

Add the broccoli and the mushrooms and let them cook slowly in about 15 minutes. Stir regularly or the sauce will cook.

After an hour, remove the chicken from the sous vide bath and pat them dry with kitchen paper. Then make a pan piping hot and fry the chicken on both sides for a nice brown layer. Serve immediately.

Combine the chicken with the broccoli cheese sauce. Enjoy your meal!

- **Mashed potatoes at 72 degrees**

Ingredients for 6 portions

- 1 kilo of potato
- 250 grams of butter
- 150 grams of milk

Preparation

Total time approx. 90 minutes

Peel the potatoes. When the beepers are out of their jacket, cut them into equal parts about 1 centimeter thick; in this way all potatoes are cooked at the same time. Save the peels.

And as a final step in preparation, wash your potatoes for a long time! By cutting into the potato, you break cell walls in the potato, so that starch is released on the cutting surface. If you were to cook your potatoes immediately, all this starch would end up in the cooking liquid, which does not make the mash better. Rinse the potatoes well for a few minutes, so that all the starch in your sink has disappeared.

If you were to put the washed potatoes in boiling water, the cell walls would burst and you would lose part of the starch. With a simple trick you can ensure that the starch is first fixed in the potato. As a result, the potato loses less starch during further preparation, exactly what we want!

And how do you do that? Simply put your potatoes in 72 degree water for 30 minutes, easily done via sous vide. Really. It makes your potato a different potato… It is not cooked, but feels firm. All the starch is now well locked in the potato.

The potato has the most flavor in the skin. And a shame not to use it in your mash! To get that done, wash the skins thoroughly and bring them to the boil while stirring with the milk. Remove the pan from the heat as soon as the milk boils and let it rest until use. This draws the taste of the skins into the milk, which you finally add to your puree.

Rinse the potatoes well again after 30 minutes and cook them fully cooked for another 30 minutes. This is of course possible without sous vide and simply by boiling the water.

Cut the butter into pieces and put them in a mixing bowl. Drain the boiled potatoes and squeeze them finely with the puree squeezer (or alternatively use a puree mash). Stir the butter-potato mixture well.

Now rub the puree through the finest possible (baker's) sieve.

Add a dash of milk and stir in the puree well. Keep adding milk until you have achieved the desired consistency. Season with fresh pepper and sea salt. The enthusiast now adds some nutmeg, or lemon / lime zest (to act as a fresh counterpart to the butter).

CONCLUSION

Is this newfangled modern cooking method really worth investing in for everyday home cooking? I will share reasons why I think sous vide is a practical tool for everything from a weeknight dinner to a fancy dinner party.

Even though this technique can seem so foreign and fussy — plastic pouches? High-tech gadgets? Who needs all that in the kitchen? But the advantages of sous vide, so well-known by restaurants, can also be enormously helpful to the home cook.

Sous vide provides down-to-the-degree control in the kitchen to deliver the most tender, flavorful food you've ever had. With this, it's super simple to get restaurant-quality results from edge to edge.

The most amazing reason for me is the simplicity and flexibility of sous vide. If you're cooking for a range of food preferences or allergies, sous vide cooking can make life easier. For example, you can cook chicken marinated in a lot of spices as well as chicken just sprinkled with salt and pepper at the same time so various categories of people will be happy!

SOUS VIDE COOKBOOK FOR BEGINNERS

50 SIMPLE RECIPES

LUIS JORDAN

INTRODUCTION

Sous vide(French) also known as low temperature long time cooking, is a method of cooking in which food is placed in a plastic pouch or a glass jar and cooked in a water bath for longer than usual cooking times (usually 1 to 7 hours, up to 72 or more hours in some cases) at a precisely regulated temperature.

Sous vide cooking is mostly done using thermal immersion circulator machines.The temperature is much lower than usually used for cooking, typically around 55 to 60 °C (130 to 140 °F) for red meat, 66 to 71 °C (150 to 160 °F) for poultry, and higher for vegetables. The intent is to cook the item evenly, ensuring that the inside is properly cooked without overcooking the outside, and to retain moisture.

Sous vide cooking is much easier than you might think, and usually involved three simple steps:

- Attach your precision cooker to a pot of water and set the time and temperature according to your desired level of doneness.
- Put your food in a sealable bag and clip it to the side of the pot.
- Finish by searing, grilling, or broiling the food to add a crispy, golden exterior layer.

With precise temperature control in the kitchen, sous vide provides the following benefits:

- Consistency. Because you cook your food to a precise temperature for a precise amount of time, you can expect very consistent results.
- Taste. Food cooks in its juices. This ensures that the food is moist, juicy and tender.
- Waste reduction. Traditionally prepared food dries out and results in waste. For example, on average, traditionally cooked steak loses

up to 40% of its volume due to drying out. Steak cooked via precision cooking, loses none of its volume.

- Flexibility. Traditional cooking can require your constant attention. Precision cooking brings food to an exact temperature and holds it. There is no worry about overcooking.

8. **Sous vide rump steak**

Ingredients for 2 portions

- 2 stk Rump steak (roast beef) a 250g
- 1 prizesalt
- 1 prizepepper
- 1 shot Oil for the pan
  Preparation

With the rump steak recipe, it is important to know in advance how you want the meat. This and the meat thickness also result in the different cooking times and cooking temperatures - see below for details.

The ideal thickness of the steaks should be between 2-3 cm and it should have a nice marbling. First wash the meat, pat dry and then vacuum each piece of meat in a suitable cooking foil.

Now put the two pieces of meat side by side in the sous vide device (or steam oven) and cook according to the desired degree of cooking - here are a few aids: Rare 47 degrees, medium 55 degrees, well done 63 degrees for approx. 70 minutes. The thicker the meat, the longer it has to be cooked - little help: 4 cm around 120 minutes, 5 cm 160 minutes.

After cooking, remove the meat, cut out of the bag, catch the juice - this can serve as the basis for a sauce - dab the meat a little, salt and pepper, and in a very hot pan with a dash of oil or butter on both sides sear hot - approx. 60-90 seconds on each side.

9. Roast beef sous vide

Ingredients for 4 portions

- 1 kg roast beef
- 1 shot olive oil
- 3 branch rosemary
- 3 branch thyme
- 20 g butter

Preparation

Total time approx. 5 hours 20 minutes

The most important thing with sous vide cooking of a meat or fish is that you have a vacuum sealer and at best a sous vide cooker.

First take the steak out of its packaging and wash it off with cold water, then dab it with crepe paper.

Please separate the thyme and rosemary leaves from the stem and do not vacuum the stem as it is too hard.

Now rub the roast beef with the olive oil and place in a plastic bag that is suitable for sous vide cooking. Then add the thyme and rosemary leaves to the bag. Vacuum everything in this bag.

Preheat the sous vide cooker to 56 degrees and add the roast beef to the water bath. The meat must then be cooked in a water bath for 5 hours.

After 5 hours, take the steak out of the bag and dab it. Heat a grill pan and sear the meat briefly on each side for a maximum of 1 minute. Put the butter in the pan to round off.

Then leave the steak on a preheated plate for 3 minutes.

10. Bison fillet with broad beans

Ingredients for 2 portions

- 1 cup polenta
- Salt and pepper, white
- 1 cup milk
- 1 cup water
- 30 g Morels, dried (black morels)
- 3 protein
- Butter
- 150 g Beans (broad beans), frozen
- 100 ml orange juice
- 1 tbsp. Tarragon, plucked leaves
- 300 g Fillet of bison
- 1 tbsp. clarified butter

Preparation

Total time approx. 30 minutes

Seal the bison fillet in a plastic bag. Let it soak in a water bath at 65 ° C
for about 2 hours. Unpack the bison fillet, season with salt and pepper
and let all sides briefly and vigorously take the color in clarified butter,
let it rest for at least 5 minutes, then cut into two slices.

Cook the polenta in a mixture of milk and water with a little salt. Soak
the morels, then cut them into small pieces and add them to the cooled
polenta. Possibly. Add the morels' soaking water to improve the
consistency. Beat the egg whites with a little salt until stiff, fold under
the polenta and pour the mixture into buttered tins. Bake in a water
bath at 180 ° C until lightly browned.

Let the broad beans thaw, remove the thick skin. Reduce the orange
juice a little, add the butter and salt. Only heat the broad beans in it
briefly. Finely chop the tarragon and add before serving.

11. Sous vide salmon fillet

Ingredients for 4 portions

- 450 g Salmon fillet, fresh
- Olive oil
- Salt and pepper
- Garlic powder
- Lemon juice

Preparation

Total time approx. 1 hour

Prepare a suitable vacuum bag, vacuum the salmon with 1 teaspoon of olive oil and a little salt. Carefully place the salmon in the vacuum bag in the water bath preheated to 52 ° C and cook for about 20 - 25 minutes.

Then take the salmon out of the bath, carefully take the fish out of the bag and fry lightly in the pan, but it can also be consumed directly.

Arrange salt and a little pepper with a little lemon juice, depending on your taste. Serve on vegetables or rice, depending on taste.

12. Beef high rib - sous vide cooked

Ingredients for 3 portions

- 4 tbsp. Worcester sauce
- 2 tbsp. salt
- 1 tbsp. Pepper, freshly ground
- 1 tbsp. rapeseed oil
- 1.3 kg Roast beef (high rib, with bone)

Preparation

Total time approx. 8 hours 30 minutes

Rub the high rib generously with the Worcestershire sauce. Then sprinkle with salt and rub in as well. Place in a vacuum bag and seal. Transfer to the Sous Vide container and cook for 8 hours at 56 ° C. When the time is up, sear the rib on all sides in a skillet or on the grill. Then cut into slices and sprinkle with freshly ground pepper.

This goes well with pan-fried vegetables and dips at your convenience.

13. Pork fillet with tarragon cream

Ingredients for 4 portions

- 1 Pork
- 1 bunchTarragon, fresher
- 1 tbsp. Mustard, gritty
- 200 ml cream
- 1 Shallot
- 1 tbsp. Sunflower oil
- 10 g butter
- Salt and pepper

Preparation

Total time approx. 1 hour 50 minutes

Wash the pork fillet, pat dry and remove excess fat and tendons. Rub with sunflower oil, salt and pepper. Wash the tarragon, shake dry and chop finely. Peel and finely dice the shallot.

Put the pork fillet in a bag, add a teaspoon of tarragon and vacuum. Cook on shelf 3 in the "Sous vide" program at 65 ° C for approx. 80 minutes in the steam cooker.

115

In the meantime, sweat the shallot cubes in the butter until translucent and then deglaze with the cream. Stir in the mustard, add the remaining tarragon and let it simmer a little.

When the pork fillet is cooked, it is fried in a very hot pan. When the sous vide meat has been cooked, it has no crust. In order not to change the cooking point significantly during roasting, the pan must be very hot so that the crust forms very quickly. Carve the pork at an angle and arrange on the tarragon cream.

14. Cod-sous-vide

Ingredients for 2 portions

- 2 Cod fillet
- 2 tbsp. Parsley, dried
- 4 tbsp. olive oil
- 2 toes garlic
- 1 teaspoon lemon juice
- Salt and pepper

Preparation

Total time approx. 30 minutes

Make a marinade from olive oil, parsley, pressed garlic, lemon juice, salt and pepper.

Prepare two vacuum bags. Spread the marinade on the fish fillets and weld the fillets with the vacuum device.

Cook for 20 minutes at 52 degrees.

Tip: Swirl the cooked fish quickly in a pan with hot butter.

15. Sous-vide cooked pork belly

Ingredients for 2 portions

- 500 g Boneless pork belly
- 30 g Pickling salt (nitrite pickling salt)
- 15 g Sugar, brown
- 1 Bay leaf
- 10 Juniper berry
- 10 peppercorns
- 3 Clove
- 2 tbsp. Mustard medium hot
- Pepper, black, coarsely ground

Preparation

Boil 300 ml of water with pickling salt and brown sugar in a saucepan to a pickle brine. Let the brine cool down and vaccinate the meat with a brine syringe.

Crush the juniper berries and peppercorns and add to the rest of the brine with the bay leaf and cloves. Place the pork belly with the brine in a freezer bag, close tightly and leave in the fridge for 12 hours.

Remove the meat, wash off, dry, season with pepper and brush with mustard. Vacuum the pork belly and cook in a water bath at 65 degrees for 24 hours.

When the cooking time is over, remove the meat from the vacuum bag, cut the rind into a diamond shape and fry until crispy under the grill in the oven. Cut the pork belly into slices and serve with sauerkraut and mashed potatoes.

16. Duck roll sous-vide

Ingredients for 6 portions

- 2 Club (duck)
- 1 duck breast
- Bacon, fatter
- 50 g Pistachios, roughly chopped
- 80 g Macadamia nuts, roughly chopped
- 2 small ones Egg
- Cream
- Salt
- Pepper
- 150 g Bacon
- Pepper,
- Sea salt

  Preparation

  Total time approx. 1 hour 40 minutes

Remove the skin from the duck legs and breast, dice very finely and slowly fry them in a pan until they are crispy. Then place on a sieve to drain.

Release the duck legs and prepare a stock from the bones

Cut the duck breast into strips

Finely dice the bacon.

Make a farce from the meat of the legs, cream, eggs, spices and bacon. Mix the pistachios and nuts and part of the roasted duck skin under the farce.

Lay the bacon overlapping on a board and spread the farce on it, spread the strips of duck breast over the farce. Roll everything up with the bacon.

Put the roll in a vacuum bag and cook at 60 ° for about 1 hour.

Take the roll out of the bag and briefly fry it all around in the duck fat, cut it into slices for serving and sprinkle with the roasted duck skin and some freshly ground Tasmanian pepper and fleur de sel.

17. Pork saddle sous vide

Ingredients for 4 portions

- 800 g Pork
- 2 toes garlic
- 3 tbsp. butter
- 1 Bay leaf
- Olive oil
- Pepper, black from the mill
- Salt

Preparation

Total time approx. 2 hours 20 minutes

Rub the back piece with a little olive oil and cover with garlic slices and the bay leaf and vacuum.

Place in a 60 ° warm water bath for approx. 75 - 90 minutes. Alternatively, you can also use the steamer.

Time is of secondary importance, as the meat cannot get warmer than 60 °. It's better to leave it in longer if you're unsure.

Then take out the pork, let the butter froth in a hot pan and briefly fry the meat in it. Season with salt and pepper and cut open.

This goes with risotto and roasted vegetables (e.g. pointed peppers). The meat is then very tender, light pink and very tasty.

18. Sous vide cooked leg of lamb

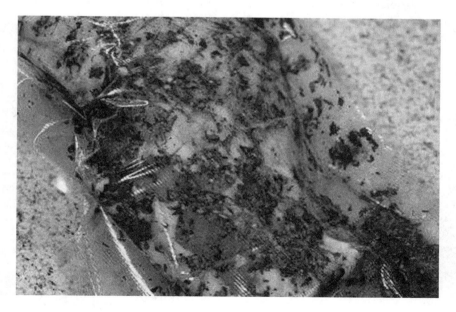

Ingredients for 6 portions

For the marinade:

- 1 handful Pepper, black
- 1 handful salt
- 1 tuber garlic
- 1 bunchcoriander
- 2 Shallot
- 1 Lime

For the meat:

- 1 Leg of lamb, with bone, 2 - 3 kg
- 1 handful salt

Preparation

Total time approx. 18 hours 30 minutes

Wrap the bulb of garlic in aluminum foil and roast on the grill or in the oven at 180 ° C for one hour.

For the marinade, finely grind salt and pepper in a mortar. Halve the roasted and now soft garlic and squeeze half into the mortar. Chop the coriander and shallots and add to the mortar. Squeeze the lime, add the juice to the mortar and mix everything into a suspension.

Fill a sous vide water bath and preheat to 58 ° C.

Parry the leg of lamb. If it has a strong grease cap, peel it off a little. Cut the fat cap into a diamond shape, being careful not to injure the meat. Salt the leg, rub it with the marinade, add the remaining garlic and vacuum the leg. Cook sous vide for 18 hours (this is not a typo).

After cooking, remove the leg from the bag and pat dry. Grill on the grill in direct heat to create roasted aromas.

19. Confined duck legs sous-vide

Ingredients for 2 portions

- 2 Duck leg
- Sea-salt
- Pepper, black, freshly ground
- 1 tbsp. Duck stock, concentrated
- 2 Bay leaves, fresh
- 5 grainspimento
- 3 disc Garlic, dried
- 2 tbsp. Heaped Lard (duck), chilled

Preparation

Total time approx. 3 days 8 hours 5 minutes

Rub the duck legs with the duck stock and salt and pepper well.
Vacuum together with the other ingredients in a bag (since some liquid
is sucked in with a household vacuum sealer, check the weld seam
carefully for leaks) and cook at 80 ° C for eight hours, then cool down
quickly in an ice water bath for at least 15 minutes.

Leave in the fridge for a few days or longer if possible.

To serve in a water bath, heat at 75 to 80 ° C, carefully remove from the bag and, if necessary, brown the skin briefly under the salamander or the infrared grill of the oven.

20. Asparagus with red curry

Ingredients for 2 portions

- 500 g Asparagus, white
- 2 Tea spoons Curry paste, red
- 3 tbsp. Coconut milk, frozen
- 1 pinch sugar
- 1 pinch salt
- 1 teaspoon butter

Preparation

Total time approx. 55 minutes

Buy fresh asparagus and peel it clean.

Then season the asparagus with salt and sugar - put in a bag. Then distribute the remaining ingredients in the bag. Spread the curry paste a little over the asparagus. I like to use frozen coconut milk for the sous vide method. I usually need small amounts so that I always have some coconut milk in the ice cube container and can vacuum it more easily.

Set the water bath to 85 ° C and cook the asparagus for 45 minutes.

Open the bag at the end of the cooking time. Catch the juice from asparagus water, curry and coconut milk, thicken a little and serve with the asparagus.

21. Boiled fillet

Ingredients for 4 portions

- 1 kg Beef
- 1 Carrot
- 50 g celery root
- 1 small Onion
- 1 tbsp. oil
- 100 ml White wine
- Sea-salt
- 6 peppercorns
- 1 Bay leaf

Preparation

Total time approx. 20 hours 15 minutes

Peel the skin off the top of the boiled beef. Dice the carrot, onion and celery finely. Heat the oil in a pan and sweat the vegetables. Deglaze with white wine, reduce it almost completely.

Rub the boiled fillet with a little oil, salt (not too much) and put in a vacuum bag. Add vegetables, bay leaf and peppercorns and distribute in the bag. Vacuuming. Cook in a water bath at 60 to 65 ° C for 20 hours.

Then take out of the bag, remove the vegetables and cut the boiled beef.

The meat becomes tender, aromatic and retains an even pink color. Tastes delicious with breadcrumbs, green sauce or on root vegetables.

The right temperature is a bit a matter of taste. I always cook it at 64 ° C. The longer it stays in it, the more the structure of the meat is lost. One more day and it can be crushed with the tongue. I like it a little "crisper".

The amount per serving is already quite generous, one can eat more with it.

22. Vanilla chicken with honey carrots

Ingredients for 2 portions

- 2 Chicken breast fillet, without skin
- ½ Vanilla bean, halved lengthways
- 2 tbsp. Oil, grape seed
- 16 Carrot, baby, peeled
- 2 tbsp. butter
- 3 tbsp. Acacia honey
- Salt
- Pepper, black, ground

Preparation

Total time approx. 4 hours

Vacuum the chicken breast fillets with the oil, vanilla pod and pepper and marinate for at least 2 hours.

Vacuum each 8 carrots with 1 tbsp. butter and 1.5 tbsp. honey.

Cook the chicken at 60 ° for 100 minutes in a water bath or steam cooker. Take out of the bag and sear in a preheated pan. Then salt.

Cook the carrots at 85 ° for 25 minutes in a steam oven or water bath. Then put in a preheated pan and fry until the honey has caramelized. Salt and pepper.

Arrange on preheated plates.

Goes well with couscous or polenta.

23. Sous vide beef steak with red wine

Ingredients for 2 portions

- 2 Beef steak (hip steak), approx. 250 g each
- 4 branch rosemary

- 4 branch thyme
- 100 ml port wine
- 150 ml red wine
- Olive oil, good
- Clarified butter
- Sea salt, coarse
- Pepper (steak pepper)
- 1 tsp, heaped sugar
- 1 tbsp. Butter, cold

Preparation

Total time approx. 2 hours

Pat the beef steaks dry and vacuum them with a sprig of thyme and rosemary and a small dash of olive oil.

Heat the sous vide bath to 56 degrees and then put the bags in it.

Shortly before the end of the cooking time, let the sugar caramelize in a saucepan and deglaze with the red wine and the port wine. Add the remaining herbs and let the wine simmer gently.

After 90 minutes, remove the steaks from the water bath. Place a pan with clarified butter and let the butter get really hot. In the meantime, pat the steaks lightly. Sear the steaks in the butter briefly for about 5 - 10 seconds on each side, then wrap in aluminum foil and keep warm.

Put the wine mixture in the pan and reduce to 1/3, season with salt and pepper and thicken with a little butter.

Put the sauce on the plate and put the steak on top, sprinkle with the coarse salt and pepper.

Baked potatoes go very well with this.

24. Salmon sous vide cooked

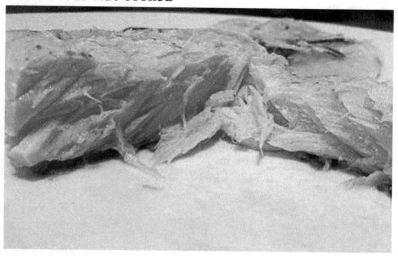

Ingredients for 1 portions

- 200 g Salmon fillet with skin
- 2 Lemon slice, thinly sliced
- 2 branch dill
- ½ Clove of garlic, thinly sliced
- Rosemary
- Thyme
- 2 dropsolive oil
- Pepper

Preparation

Total time approx. 45 minutes

Dab the salmon. Brush lightly with olive oil and pepper. Place in a sous vide bag. Spread the lemon and garlic slices as well as the herbs on the fish and vacuum everything.

Heat a water bath with a sous vide stick to 45 ° C and cook the bag with its contents for approx. 30 minutes. After 30 minutes, take the salmon out of the packaging.

Approximately Put in a hot pan on the skin side for 10 seconds and fry very hot, serve immediately.

Everyone can then season to taste with salt, pepper, lemon and chili.

25. Pork belly sous vide

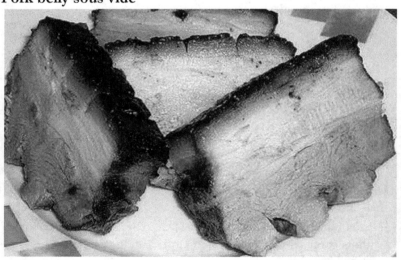

Ingredients for 2 portions

- 500 g Pork belly, uncured
- 1 Bay leaf, fresh

- 3 Juniper berry
- Salt
- Pepper, black, from the mill

Preparation

Total time approx. 15 hours 5 minutes

Divide the bay leaf into pieces. Squeeze the juniper berries. Rub the pork belly with a little salt, pepper it gently and put it in a vacuum bag with juniper berries and bay leaves.

Vacuum and cook in a water bath at 75 ° C for 15 hours.

The result is a pork belly that is tender, aromatic and juicy, but no longer pink.

26. Whole beef fillet after sous vide

Ingredients for 4 portions

- 500 g Beef fillet, whole
- 1 branch rosemary
- 2 tbsp. butter
- 2 Tea spoons salt
- 1 teaspoon Black pepper
- 3 Juniper berry
- Some Rosemary needles

Preparation

Total time approx. 3 hours 15 minutes

Wash the whole beef fillet, pat dry with kitchen paper and slowly bring it to room temperature (take it out of the fridge about 2 hours beforehand).

Then weld in foil with the sprig of rosemary.

The bowl of the Cooking Chef up to max. Fill the marking with water and set it to 58 ° C (put on splash guard, stirring interval 3 without stirrer).

When the temperature is reached, add the welded fillet of beef and leave it there for 3 hours. Close the splash guard so that the temperature remains constant!

Then take out of the CC and cut open the film.

Heat the butter with the salt, pepper, pressed juniper berries and a few rosemary needles in the pan and let it brown slightly. Briefly brown the fillet on both sides (all in all approx. 1 min.).

Just cut open (not too thin slices) and serve.

27. Rump steak à la with ciabatta

Ingredients for 1 portions

- 300 g Beef
- 1 pack arugula
- 100 g pine nuts
- 2 Garlic cloves
- 100 g Parmesan
- 150 ml olive oil
- 1 Ciabatta for baking
- 50 g Cherry tomato
- 1 ball Mozzarella
- Salt and pepper

Preparation

Total time approx. 1 hour 55 minutes

Vacuum the beef fillet and let it sit for 10-15 min. let it rest at room temperature. Warm the water to 56 ° C and place the fillet in the water bath at a constant temperature. Approximately Cook in a water bath for 50 - 55 minutes.

Meanwhile, bake the bread according to the package instructions.

138

Prepare the pesto - mix rocket, pine nuts, parmesan and oil until you get a creamy mixture. Cut the mozzarella and tomatoes into small cubes.

Cut the bread into slices and brush with the pesto. Place the tomato and mozzarella pieces on the coated slices.

Heat a pan and sear the fillet steak in it. Serve sprinkled with salt and pepper.

28. Chicken thigh sous vide

Ingredients for 1 portions
- 1 large chicken thighs
- Paprika
- Salt and pepper

Preparation

Total time approx. 1 hour 40 minutes

Rub the chicken leg with pepper, salt and paprika and seal it in a vacuum bag. If necessary, there is also a freezer bag with a slide closure, in which you suck out the air with a straw.

Heat a water bath to 82 ° C and place the vacuum bag in the water bath and cook the chicken leg for about 90 minutes at a constant 82 ° C. It doesn't matter any longer.

When the cooking time is reached, preheat a grill pan at the highest level, and also set the large grill in the oven to the highest level plus the grill program.

Take the chicken thigh out of the vacuum bag and place in the heated pan. Place the pan immediately under the grill and grill the leg in the oven for 2-4 minutes until the skin is crispy. The leg is cooked through to the last bone and has a nice grill aroma.

29. Sous-vide chamois leg

Ingredients for 2 portions

- 500 g Chamois leg, boneless, prepared by the butcher
- 200 ml Red wine, dry

- 200 ml Wild fund
- 6 Date, without stone
- 2 tbsp. Apple Cider Vinegar
- 2 tbsp. clarified butter
- 2 Onion, red
- 1 teaspoon Venison Seasoning

Preparation

Total time approx. 2 hours 40 minutes

Fry the leg of chamois in clarified butter. Allow the leg to cool down a little and then seal it in foil. Cook in a water bath at 68 degrees for about 2 hours.

Cut the onions into sticks, chop half of the dates, cut the other half into slices.

Slowly sauté the onion in the frying pan of the leg. Add the chopped dates. Deglaze with red wine, wild jus and apple cider vinegar and reduce to half. Add the game spice and the date slices.

30. Wrong filet sous vide cooked

Ingredients for 4 portions

- 1 kg Beef shoulder (false fillet)
- 2 tbsp. butter
- 2 Tea spoons thyme
- 1 teaspoon Black pepper
- 2 Garlic cloves

Preparation

Total time approx. 2 hours 30 minutes

Unpack the fillet and pat dry. Parry the meat cleanly. Rub with the butter so that the pepper and thyme stick better. Place the fillet with the pressed garlic in a vacuum bag and vacuum.

Place the wrong fillet in the sous vide device at 54 ° C and leave it there for two hours.

After two hours, open the bag and grill on all sides for 2-3 minutes on direct heat. After grilling, let the meat rest for about 3 - 5 minutes, after which it is ready.

Finely sliced, for example as a starter, absolutely delicious.

31. Beef sirloin cooked sous vide

Ingredients for 2 portions

- 600 g beef
- 1 pinch salt
- 1 pinch pepper
- 2 tbsp. Heaped oil
- 1 small Piece Butter or herb butter

Preparation

Total time approx. 1 hour 29 minutes

You take 2 300 gram beef loins, ideally from the butcher. You can either vacuum them up at the butcher or do it yourself at home, also with herbs.

Heat a pot of water and then wait for it to boil. Don't forget to put the lid on it. As soon as the water boils properly, it has a temperature of approx. 100 degrees.

You put the pot with the lid off the hob and wait about 5 minutes. Then the water has a temperature between 85 and 90 degrees. Now put the meat in the vacuum bag in the water until it is covered. Put the lid back on and let simmer for 15 minutes.

With this we reach a core temperature of approx. 50 degrees in the meat. After this time, take it out of the pot and let it rest for 4-5 minutes.

Now the meat comes out of its bag. You massage it with oil and season it with salt and pepper on each side. Let the pan heat up at the same time and then sear the end of the rendition, approx. 1.5 minutes per side. Now remove the pan from the hob and add a piece of (herb) butter. So that the meat rub in from all sides and let the meat rest again.

Now arrange on the plate and pour over the remaining herb butter if necessary.

32. Potatoes with fermented yuzu

Ingredients for 4 portions

- 700 g Potato, firm-cooking
- 50 g celery
- 50 g Carrot
- 1 Shallot
- 10 g Yuzu, fermented
- 20 ml vegetable stock
- 1 pinch sugar
- Soy Sauce

Preparation

Total time approx. 2 hours 35 minutes

Peel the potatoes, cut into cubes (approx. 2 cm edge size), blanch briefly in salt water and let cool.

Cut the celery, carrots and shallots into very fine cubes.

Put all the ingredients in a vacuum bag together with the fermented yuzu, the vegetable broth and a pinch of sugar. Apply a medium vacuum and cook at 85 ° C for about 2 hours.

Then open the bag and season with a little yuzu soy.

33. White asparagus sous vide

Ingredients for 2 portions
- 800 g Asparagus, white

- 1 teaspoon sugar
- 1 pinch salt
- 50 g butter
- Herbs

Preparation

Total time approx. 40 minutes

Peel the asparagus and cut off the ends. Put the asparagus spears in a bag, add salt, sugar and butter and vacuum.

Cook on shelf 3 in the "Sous vide" program at 85 ° C for approx. 30 minutes in the steam cooker.

If you like, you can vacuum herbs such as basil, wild garlic, thyme, rosemary or mint with the asparagus. But watch out! The taste experience becomes quite intense.

34. Wild goose breast sous vide

Ingredients for 4 portions

- 2 Goose breasts triggered by wild geese
- 2 Tea spoons Salt, coarse
- 1 teaspoon Peppercorns, black
- 6 Juniper berry
- 3 Allspice
- 200 ml walnut oil
- 100 ml red wine
- 200 ml Wild fund
- Cornstarch for setting

Preparation

Total time approx. 1 hour 25 minutes

Mortar the spices. Place 1 breast each in a vacuum bag. Add 100 ml of nut oil to each bag. Vacuum and cook in a water bath at 68 degrees for about 1 hour.

Then remove, pat dry and fry all around in the pan. Let it rest a little and then cut.

In the meantime, deglaze the roast with red wine and let it boil down a little. Pour in the game stock, possibly season with salt, pepper and sugar and then tie with cornstarch.

35. Rabbit sous-vide

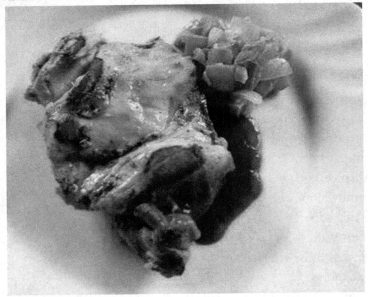

Ingredients for 4 portions

- 4 Rabbit leg
- 1 Onion
- 3 Carrot
- 1 bar leek

- 1 Garlic cloves
- 1 smaller celery root
- Rosemary
- 2 tbsp. olive oil
- Salt and pepper

Preparation

Total time approx. 3 hours 30 minutes

Wash the rabbit legs and rub dry with kitchen paper. Release the bones and season the meat with salt and pepper.

Peel the onion, clove of garlic, carrots and celery and cut into small cubes. Cut the leek into strips. Sweat everything in a saucepan with 1 tablespoon of olive oil for 3 minutes and let cool. Add the rosemary at will. Place the legs and vegetables in a vacuum bag and vacuum.

Cook the rabbit legs in the sous vide device at 65 degrees for 3 hours.

Let the stock from the bag reduce a little and put in a gravy. Fry the legs in the remaining olive oil. Arrange the vegetables from the bag on the plates.

36. Leg of lamb sous vide

Ingredients for 4 portions

- 1 kg Leg of lamb, boned
- Salt and pepper
- 1 branch rosemary
- 1 tbsp. clarified butter

Preparation

Total time approx. 19 hours

Salt and pepper the boned leg of lamb normally from all sides, place a sprig of rosemary in the opening of the bone. Fold up the meat, place it in a suitable vacuum bag and vacuum.

Preheat the sous vide cooker to 65 ° C, insert the meat and cook at 65 ° C for 18 hours.

After the cooking time, remove the meat from the bag, dab and fry briefly and vigorously in clarified butter. Keep warm at 65 ° C or weld in again and reheat at 65 ° C in the sous vide pot if necessary.

The meat is just through and tender.

37. Crocodile fillets sous-vide

Ingredients for 4 portions

- 500 g Filet (crocodile fillets)
- 1 Lemons
- 1 tbsp. lemon oil
- 3 tbsp. olive oil
- 4 Spring onion, cut into fine rings
- ½ Lemon, the juice of it
- Pepper
- Salt
- 1 branch rosemary

Preparation

Total time approx. 4 hours 30 minutes

Wash the fillets and pat dry.

Mix all the ingredients for the marinade together. Place the fillets in the bags and cover with the marinade. Cut the whole lemon into thin slices and place on the fillets.

Seal the Sous-vide bags, if possible, refrigerate for 1 - 2 hours. Cook softly in a sous vide cooker at 80 ° C for 3 hours.

153

Take the fillets out of the bags and roughly scrape them off. Heat up a large pan with plenty of butter.
Only sear briefly on high heat so that the fillets turn golden brown.
Serve immediately.
A lemon and quince sauce goes well with this.

38. Salmon with cream cheese

Ingredients for 2 portions

- 250 g Salmon, frozen
- 200 g double cream
- 2 cup Basmati
- 4 cup water
- 1 Lemons
- 1 curry powder

Preparation

Total time approx. 45 minutes

When the salmon is thawed, pat them a little dry and then season them. Then it comes in Sous Vide vacuum bags.

Set the vacuum sealer with a fish thickness of approx. 1.5 - 2 cm to 55 ° C for 15 minutes. The fish is still glassy and not dry afterwards, and tastes great.

Basically, it is important with basmati rice that it is soaked for about 15 minutes, depending on the amount. Then it should be rinsed thoroughly until the water becomes clear and is no longer milky. Then it must be prepared according to the manufacturer's instructions. mix the basmati rice with a little lemon zest after cooking, it tasted very refreshing!

Simply mixed the cream cheese with a little lemon zest and curry powder. Tasted very good and went well with the salmon.

39. Goose leg sous vide

Ingredients for 4 portions

- 4 Goose leg
- 2 Orange
- 2 apples
- Salt and pepper

Preparation

Total time approx. 1 day 8 hours 40 minutes

Season the goose legs with salt and pepper. Cut the peel from the oranges and cut into slices. Wash the apples, quarter them, remove the core and cut them into small pieces.

Place the goose legs, the oranges and the apples in a vacuum bag and vacuum. Place in the fridge for 1 day so that the goose legs can pull through.

Put the legs with the fruit in the sous vide cooker and let them stand for 6 hours at 70 degrees. Then let it steep for another 2 hours at 80 degrees.

Remove the legs from the bag and bake until crispy in the oven at 200 degrees. Put the stock, the oranges and the apples in a pre-made sauce, mix and pass.

In addition, bread dumplings, red cabbage and glazed chestnuts taste great.

40. Goose breast sous vide

Ingredients for 2 portions

- ½ Goose breast, approx. 300 g
- Salt and pepper
- Paprika powder, noble sweet
- Clarified butter
- 1 Shallot
- Geese fund

Preparation

Total time approx. 12 hours 20 minutes

Rub the boneless goose breast with the spices, vacuum in the bag and cook in a water bath at 65 degrees for 12 hours.

Then take the goose breast out of the bag. Collect the cooking liquid.

Let the clarified butter get very hot in a pan. Roast the goose breasts briefly and sharply on the side of the house, briefly so that they do not post-cook, take them out and keep them warm.

Chop the shallot finely, sauté in a roast set, pour in the cooking liquid and possibly goose stock, let it boil down a little, then bind with sauce binder or butter as you like.

158

41. Roast beef dry aged, sous vide

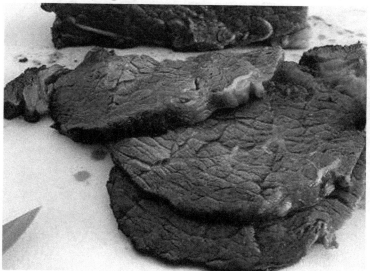

Ingredients for 4 portions

- 800 g Roast beef dry aged, in one piece
- Spice at will

Preparation

Total time approx. 7 hours 30 minutes

Clean the roast beef and seal it in a vacuum bag. Heat the water to 52 degrees (medium rare) with a Sous vide Stick, leave the meat in a water bath for about 7 hours.

Remove the vacuum bag and add the meat juice to the side dish (if desired).

Season the meat and fry all around in a pan. Cut into slices approx. 1 cm thick and arrange.

42. Salmon trout on a bed of vegetables

Ingredients for 4 portions

- 1 large Salmon trout filleted on 4 pieces, the carcasses save for the rear
- 50 g Celery, finely chopped
- 50 g Carrot, finely chopped
- 50 g Leek, finely chopped
- 2 stripsPeel the orange peel, wide, 2 times with the peeler
- Parsley
- Tarragon
- Some orange zest
- 200 ml fish stock
- 60 ml Vinegar, light, sweet (apple balsamic vinegar)
- 10 Peppercorns, white
- 4 Allspice
- 40 ml White wine
- 60 ml Noilly Prat
- 4 tbsp. Coconut milk, the solid ingredient
- 2 cm ginger

- 2 stemsLemongrass, in pieces
- 5 Kaffir lime leaves
- 3 large ones Sweet potato
- 2 m. In size Potato
- Rear
- Salt and pepper

Preparation

Total time approx. 2 hours 50 minutes

First fillet the salmon trout and peel off the skin. Pull out the bones with a pair of fish tongs and lightly season the fillets on the inside with salt and pepper. Then cover the inside with parsley, tarragon and orange zest and set the fillets aside.

Bring the fish stock to the boil with vinegar, white wine, Noilly Prat, coconut milk, the spices (allspice, pepper, ginger, lemon grass, kaffir lime leaves) and the fish carcasses and reduce them by about 15 - 20 minutes.

Meanwhile, lightly fry the vegetable strips with the orange peel in a little clarified butter and season with salt and pepper.

Put some vegetables in suitable vacuum bags, put a fillet on each and pour some stock. Then seal the bags with a vacuum device.

Peel the sweet potatoes and potatoes, cut them into pieces and steam them in the steamer for about 30 minutes. Then press through a potato press and season with a thickened stock, salt and pepper and keep warm.

Cook the fish fillets in a water bath at 56 ° C for 18 minutes.

Place a sweet potato purée on preheated plates, cut open a sack, drape the contents on the mirrors and cover with fish stock. Decorate as desired.

43. Rabbit back and legs with stock

Ingredients for 2 portions

- 1 Rabbit back or 2 rabbit fillets
- 2 Rabbit leg (rabbit thigh)
- 4 tbsp.Butter, cold
  For the lake:
- 1 teaspoon Juniper berry
- 1 teaspoon peppercorns
- 2 branch thyme
- Salt
  For the fund:
- 1 Rabbit's back, including the bones
- 1 small bowl vegetable soup
- 1 Onion
- 2 tbsp. oil
- 1 Bay leaf
- 1 tsp. peppercorns
  For the sauce: (Demi-Glace)
- 1 tbsp. butter
- 2 Shallot

- 1 tsp, heaped tomato paste
- 250 ml Red wine, drier
- 150 ml port wine
- 2 branch thyme
- 50 g butter

Preparation

Total time approx. 1 day 9 hours 45 minutes

Place the meat in a flavored brine for 24 hours. This means that the meat remains juicier, retains a pleasant bite, is optimally salted and is slightly flavored.

Weigh the meat and cover it with at least the same weight of water. Add 1.75% of the total weight of meat and water to salt and dissolve in the water. Press on the juniper berries and pepper and add to the water with the thyme. If necessary, weigh down with a plate to keep the pieces of meat down.

Take the rabbit legs out of the brine and pat dry. Add the butter and vacuum the thighs. Cook sous vide for 8 hours at 75 ° C. The rabbit legs can then be fried in a little butter or boned and processed further.

Remove the back fillets from the brine and pat dry. Approximately Place 30 cm cling film on the worktop. Place the fillets on top of each other in opposite directions. Place the thin end on the thick end and the thick end on the thin end so that a uniform strand is created. Fold the cling film over and twist the ends so that an even roll is created. The fillets must be pressed tightly together so that they hold together after cooking. Secure the ends of the roll with yarn, place the roll in a vacuum bag and vacuum. Cook sous vide for 45 minutes at 58 ° C. The back fillet roulade can be cut and served nicely after cooking. Searing is not necessary.

Preheat the oven to 220 ° C for the rear. Chop the bones into pieces. Clean the soup vegetables, apart from parsley, and chop them roughly. Quarter the onion. Mix vegetables and oil and roast in the oven for approx. 30 - 45 minutes until you get a nice tan. Possibly stir well after half the time. Put the vegetables and bones in a large saucepan. Remove the roast residues from the tray with a little water and add. Add bay leaf, peppercorns and parsley. Fill up with approx. 2 l of water, bring to a boil and simmer for 1.5 - 2 hours. The cooking time can be reduced accordingly in the pressure cooker. Strain the stock and squeeze the vegetables and bones well. There should be about 1 liter left.

For the Demi-Glace, dice the shallots and braise until translucent with a little butter. Add the tomato paste and roast for a few minutes. Gradually add the wine and port wine and let it boil down almost completely. Add the rabbit stock and thyme and let it boil down slowly until the sauce becomes creamy. If it is to be served immediately, tie it with ice-cold butter. If you prefer to bind with flour, you can brown the butter in a separate saucepan until it smells nutty, add 1 tablespoon of flour and toast briefly. Be careful not to burn the butter. Top up with the sauce and stir constantly so that no lumps form. The bound sauce can be reheated well.

44. Greek salad sous vide

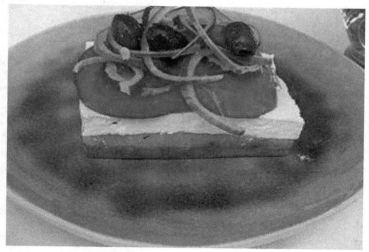

Ingredients for 2 portions

- 1 Cucumber
- 2 Tea spoons Balsamic vinegar, white
- 3 tsp sugar
- 2 stemsdill
- 1 large Tomatoes
- 200 g feta cheese
- ½ Onion, red
- 6 Olives
- Olive oil, good

Preparation

Total time approx. 1 day 15 minutes

Peel the cucumber and cut it into three parts. Vacuum the cucumber pieces with balsamic vinegar, sugar and dill. Let rest in the fridge for 24 hours.

The next day, cut the cucumber into suitable strips and place it in the middle of the plate. Cut the sheep's cheese into the same size and place on the cucumber. Then cut the tomato into slices and put on the sheep cheese. Sprinkle a little pepper on the tomato. Finally, place the onion in thin strips on the turret. Garnish with the olives and pour olive oil over the salad as desired.

165

By vacuuming the cucumber gets a much more intense taste. Time is worth it.

45. Beef sous-vide picanha style

Ingredients for 4 portions

- 1.2 kg Beef
- 3 tbsp. olive oil
- 3 branch rosemary
- 1 clarified butter
- Salt and pepper

Preparation

Total time approx. 1 day 1 hour

As far as possible, the boiled fillet should still have the 0.5-1 cm thick layer of fat, as with a Brazilian picanha. This is cut into a diamond shape without cutting into the meat.

Place the meat with the olive oil and the stripped rosemary needles in a vacuum bag, vacuum seal and seal. Do not add salt. Heat in the thermalizer at 56 degrees for 24 hours. Remove the meat after the cooking time, catch some of the gravy that has formed. This can be added to a prepared red wine sauce, for example.

Sear the meat in clarified butter from all sides, season with pepper and salt. Cut into approx. 1 cm thick slices across the grain. The inside of the meat is pink (medium).

There are, for example, bacon beans, chanterelles and croquettes or potato gratin

46. Pulled pork sous vide in asia style

Ingredients for 3 portions

- 1½ kg Pork neck without bones
- 2½ tsp Five-spice powder
- ¼ cup hoisin sauce
- 3 tbsp. soy sauce
- 3 tbsp. honey
- 2 tbsp. Rice wine (Shaoxing rice wine)
- 2 tbsp. Ginger, fresher, grated
- 2 tbsp. Garlic, pressed
- 1 Lemon, peel thereof

Preparation

Total time approx. 20 hours 35 minutes

You need a sous vide cooker, a vacuum device and a vacuum bag. I suppose you can use a very dense freezer bag, but I wouldn't really trust the density.

If you have got the pork neck with bone, you either have to remove it or put two bags on top of each other for sous vide cooking so that the bone does not cut a hole in the bag and water gets into it.

Either leave the pork neck whole or cut it into rough cubes. The advantage of the previous cutting is that the length of the meat fibers is already determined.

Mix the remaining ingredients for the marinade auce together.

Now cut a bag into a sufficiently large size for sous-vide cooking and be generous. Already weld a seam with the vacuum sealer and put the meat in the opening of the bag.

Pour in the sauce and vacuum the bag - being careful not to remove the sauce.

Put enough water in the sous vide cooker at 70 ° C. When the temperature is reached, put the bag in so that it is completely submerged. Tip: I always add hot water to save time. Leave the meat in a water bath for 20 - 24 hours.

In the meantime, be sure to check whether there is still enough liquid and, above all, whether the bag is floating off the meat due to the development of steam. If so, you have to complain and press under the surface. Cutlery, tongs, etc. can be used for this - just nothing, please, that keeps the water away from the meat, such as plates and the like.

Optional: For a light crust, preheat the oven to maximum temperature and grill or top heat.

After cooking, remove the bag, cut a small corner and pour the leaked liquid into a saucepan. Remove the meat from the bag. Now it is theoretically finished and can be picked up.

Or for a light crust, pat the meat dry on the outside. Place in a large ovenproof dish and grill in the oven until a light crust has formed. Then shred the meat in a large bowl. That should be very easy. Now add the zest of the lemon.

Try the meat: if it is too dry, add some of the liquid. Otherwise, gently boil down the leaked liquid on the stove.

To do this, you have to use a heat-resistant silicone spatula to stir constantly and move the sauce at the bottom of the pot, because the liquid contains honey and hoisin sauce - both tend to burn.

When the desired consistency is achieved, the sauce can be added to the meat and mixed in, or served separately. I usually mix them in. The mixture can also be loosened up well with a little water.

This "Pulled Pork" in the Asian style is quite sweet and can now be eaten in any way: on burger rolls, in wraps, tacos, , etc.

The meat is particularly good with something crisp, as well as with a little acid, such as something inlaid. For example, I take a few cucumber slices that have been briefly soaked in a vinegar-water-sugar-salt mixture, or red onions that have been sliced with a pinch of salt and sugar, and light vinegar with a fork, or classic coleslaw. I also find corn and spring onions very nice.

Freezing works easily right after sous vide cooking. Quickly cool down, re-vacuum and freeze while still in the bag in the ice bath.

Use within about 4 weeks.

To do this, defrost the meat gently in the refrigerator over 2 days, then place it under the grill or fry it all around in the pan. This only works if the meat is cold and therefore firmer than straight from the sous vide cooker. Then pick them up and, if necessary, bring them back to full temperature in the microwave or in a saucepan.

The amount is for 4 people - from 1.5 kg after sous vide cooking approx. 1.1 kg - is generously calculated and varies depending on the purpose.

47. Egg sous-vide

Ingredients for 1 portions

17. 1 Egg, size L
18. 1 pinch salt and pepper

Preparation

I have set the sous vide stick to 62 ° C. Then place the egg or eggs in a water bath for 45 minutes.

At the temperature I set, the egg yolk is still very fluid - which is why it can also be used as a topping for pasta or other dishes. The egg yolk is firmer at approx. 68 ° C and does not run all over the plate. After cooking, quench the egg under cold water, whip with a knife and put on the plate. Refine with salt, pepper and other spices as you like.

40. Pork knuckle sous vide

Ingredients for 1 portions

- 1 Pork knuckle or knuckle of pork
- Spice at will

Preparation

Total time approx. 1 day 5 hours 20 minutes

The fresh, uncured pork knuckle, also known elsewhere as knuckle of pork or in Austria as stilts, is washed, dried and put in a vacuum bag. This is followed by spices at will. I like to use a grill spice mix of bell peppers (spicy and sweet), pepper, garlic, salt and a little sugar. Then the air is extracted as far as possible and the bag is sealed airtight. I use a vacuum device for this (it should also be possible to remove the air in another way and seal the bag securely. I have no experience with that.) Now the bag goes into a water bath for 28 hours at 70 degrees Celsius.

After the bath, the shank is removed from the pouch and the skin of the shank is cut into a diamond shape. The knuckle is placed in a saucepan and poured with the liquid from the bag. Now the rind is crispy fried in the oven at 160 degrees Celsius in about 45 minutes and a butter-tender but crispy knuckle is finished.

48. Leg of lamb sous vide

Ingredients for 6 portions

- 1 Leg of lamb, approx. 1.5 - 2 kg
- 3 Thyme branch
- 2 Rosemary
- 1 piece butter
- 2 Tea spoons garlic powder

Preparation

Total time approx. 20 hours 40 minutes

Parry the leg of lamb, rub with garlic powder, salt and pepper and put in a bag. Add 2 - 3 sprigs of thyme and rosemary (preferably a little more thyme and a little less rosemary) and a good sting of butter. Vacuum the bag and place in the water bath preheated to 57 ° C. Remove after 20 hours of cooking, remove the herbs and pat dry. Now place the leg of lamb on the grill (or oven) preheated to 300 ° C with indirect heat and grill for approx. 8 - 10 minutes.

49. Paprika vegetables sous vide

]
Ingredients for 4 portions

- 3 Bell pepper, red, yellow, green
- 1 branch rosemary
- 20 g butter
- Salt and pepper
  Preparation
  Total time approx. 1 hour 15 minutes

Peel the peppers with a peeler and cut them into bite-size pieces. Fill together with rosemary and butter in a vacuum bag and vacuum.

Place in the sous vide device at 90 ° C for approx. 60 - 90 minutes. Then remove from the bag and season with salt and pepper. The full aroma of the peppers is retained.

Suitable as a tasty accompaniment to all kinds of dishes.

50. Saffron fennel sous vide

Ingredients for 4 portions

- 2 tuberfennel
- 1 g saffron
- 100 ml poultry stock
- 20 ml olive oil
- 3 g salt

Preparation

Total time approx. 3 hours 20 minutes

Cut the fennel lengthways into approximately 6 mm thick slices. Where the leaves hang together through the stalk, the slices result.

The stems and the outer parts can be used well for a fennel cream soup.

Vacuum the slices together with the other ingredients in a vacuum bag. Cook in a water bath at 85 ° C for 3 hours.

Remove from the bags and reduce the cooking stock to approx. 1/3 of the amount.

A wonderful and effective side dish, for example with meat and fish dishes.

51. Roast beef with walnut crust

Ingredients for 4 portions

- 1 kg roast beef
- 150 g Walnuts, chopped
- 1½ tbsp. butter
- 50 g Parmesan, finely sliced
- 4 tbsp. Herbs, chopped, Mediterranean
- Salt and pepper

Preparation

Total time approx. 5 hours 30 minutes

Season the roast beef with salt and pepper first. Then weld in a vacuum. Cook the roast beef at 63 ° C using the sous vide method for about 4 - 5 hours.

In the meantime, create a crust from the walnuts, butter, parmesan, herbs, salt and pepper. It is best to put all the mixed ingredients in a freezer bag. In this you roll the ingredients flat to the required size. Then the crust goes in the fridge. Later you can cut the crust to the right size with a sharp knife including foil. Remove the foil and distribute it exactly on the meat.

Preheat the oven to 220 ° C grill function 20 minutes before serving and at the end of the cooking time.

Fry the roast beef in a very hot pan with little fat on each side for a very short time (30 seconds).

Remove the roast beef from the pan and place in a baking dish. Now put the crust on the meat. Put in the oven and take out the meat only when the crust is nice and brown. However, this does not take long, at most 5 minutes.

Now you can enjoy a perfect pink roast beef with a crust. B. with leek vegetables and spaetzle.

52. Beef fillet, without searing

Ingredients for 2 portions

- 400 g Beef fillet (center piece)
- 1 tbsp. Worcester sauce
- ½ tsp Pimentón de la Vera, mild
- 1 teaspoon Paprika powder, spicy
- 1 tsp, heaped raw cane sugar
- 1 tsp, heaped Chives, dr.

Preparation

Total time approx. 15 hours 10 minutes

Place the fillet in a vacuum bag. Mix all other ingredients and add to the bag. Rub the fillet with the ingredients in the bag. Then vacuum. It is best to let the fillet marinate overnight.

Remove the fillet from the refrigerator 2 hours before cooking. Preheat a sous vide suitable oven to 55 ° C. Place the fillet in the oven for 3 hours.

Take out of the bag, cut open and serve immediately.

53. Tuna steak on coconut spinach

Ingredients for 2 portions

- 2 Tuna steak, 250 g each
- 250 g Leaf spinach
- 1 small Piece Ginger, about 2 cm
- 1 tbsp. olive oil
- 3 tbsp. sesame oil
- 1 Shallot
- 1 tbsp, heaped Sesame seeds, toasted
- 100 ml coconut milk
- 1 toe garlic
- Salt and pepper

Preparation

Total time approx. 55 minutes

Let the spinach thaw and squeeze well. Peel and grate the ginger. Peel off the shallot and garlic and cut into small cubes.

Heat the olive oil and sauté the shallot and garlic. Add the spinach and braise for 10 minutes. Mix coconut milk, sesame oil and roasted sesame seeds together. Squeeze the grated ginger and add everything to the spinach. Season with salt and pepper.

Cook the vacuumed tuna steaks in the sous vide bath for 40 minutes at 44 degrees Celsius.

When everything is ready, unpack the tuna steaks, pat dry and sear for 30 seconds on each side. Season with salt and pepper.

54. Duck breast à l'orange

Ingredients for 2 portions

- 2 Boneless duck breasts
- 1 Orange
- 10 peppercorns
- 2 branch rosemary
- 20 g butter
- 20 g clarified butter
- 1 tbsp. soy sauce
- 1 tbsp. White wine vinegar
- 1 tbsp. honey
- 100 ml red wine

  Butter for frying

  Salt and pepper

  Preparation

  Total time approx. 2 hours 45 minutes

Wash the duck breasts, dry them and vacuum them with orange fillets, peppercorns, rosemary and butter. Place in a sous vide device at 66 degrees for 90 minutes.

Then take out of the bag. Collect and save the liquid and other contents. Remove the peppercorns. Cut the skin of the duck breasts in a diamond shape. Fry on the side of the skin until it is brown and crispy. Take the duck breasts out of the pan and keep them warm.

Put the orange, rosemary and the broth from the bag into the pan. Add soy sauce, white wine vinegar, honey and red wine and let simmer. Assemble with cold butter if necessary. Salt and pepper.

Pair with duchess potatoes and crunchy vegetables.

55. Saddle of lamb with potato gratin

Ingredients for 3 portions

- 3 Saddle of lamb, released (lamb salmon)
- 500 g Potato
- 3 Rosemary
- 1 cup Cream, approx. 200 g
- 3 Chili
- 1 Egg
- Thyme
- ⅛ Liter milk
- 3 toes garlic
- Salt and pepper
- Olive oil

Preparation
Total time approx. 1 hour 15 minutes

185

First vacuum each rack of lamb with 1 clove of garlic, 1 sprig of rosemary, a little thyme and a little olive oil. Approximately Cook for 60 min at 54 ° C sous vide.

In the meantime, peel potatoes, cut them into thin slices and park them in a baking dish.

Whisk the cream, milk and egg and season with salt and pepper. I like to eat spicy and have added 3 small chili peppers. Pour the liquid over the potatoes, spread the cheese on top and push the mold into the oven for approx. 45 min at 200 ° C.

As soon as the meat is ready, free it from the vacuum and sear it all around.

Just serve.

56. Rack of lamb

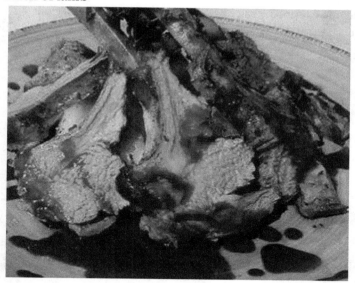

Ingredients for 4 portions

- 2 Rack of Lamb (Crown of Lamb)
- 8 Thyme branch
- 2 toes garlic
- Olive oil
- Salt and pepper

Preparation

Take the lamb crowns out of the fridge, parry and bring to room temperature.

Then place a crown in a vacuum bag and season with olive oil, salt and pepper and add 3 sprigs of thyme. Then vacuum.

If you don't have a vacuum device, you can also use the following trick: Fill

a bowl with cold water. Place the meat in a normal freezer bag and keep it under water only so far that no water can enter the opening. Then seal with a clip under water - done.

Then place the vacuumed lamb in a water bath and let it steep for about 25 minutes at 58 degrees.

Take the lamb out of the bag. Braise the remaining sprigs of thyme and the roughly chopped and crushed garlic in a pan with olive oil. Then add the lamb to the pan in one piece and briefly fry all around to obtain roasted aromas.

Then serve.

CONCLUSION

Is this newfangled modern cooking method really worth investing in for everyday home cooking? I will share reasons why I think sous vide is a practical tool for everything from a weeknight dinner to a fancy dinner party.

Even though this technique can seem so foreign and fussy — plastic pouches? High-tech gadgets? Who needs all that in the kitchen? But the advantages of sous vide, so well-known by restaurants, can also be enormously helpful to the home cook.

Sous vide provides down-to-the-degree control in the kitchen to deliver the most tender, flavorful food you've ever had. With this, it's super simple to get restaurant-quality results from edge to edge.

The most amazing reason for me is the simplicity and flexibility of sous vide. If you're cooking for a range of food preferences or allergies, sous vide cooking can make life easier. For example, you can cook chicken marinated in a lot of spices as well as chicken just sprinkled with salt and pepper at the same time so various categories of people will be happy!

CPSIA information can be obtained
at www.ICGtesting.com
Printed in the USA
BVHW010845150621
609627BV00002B/38